Making Out in Italian

Nicoletta Nencioli Aiken

D1512181

TUTTLE PUBLISHING
Tokyo • Rutland, Vermont • Singapore

Published by Tuttle Publishing, an imprint of Periplus Editions (HK) Ltd., with editorial offices at 364 Innovation Drive, North Clarendon, Vermont 05759 U.S.A. and at 61 Tai Seng Avenue #02-12, Singapore 534167.

Library of Congress Cataloging-in-Publication Data
Aiken, Nicoletta Nencioli.
  Making out in Italian / Nicoletta Nencioli Aiken.
      p. cm.
  ISBN 978-0-8048-3959-4 (pbk.)
1. Italian language--Conversation and phrase books--English. 2. Dating (Social customs)--Handbooks, manuals, etc.--Italian. I. Title.
  PC1121.A353 2008
  458.3'421--dc22

                          2008011081

ISBN 978-0-8048-3959-4

Distributed by

North America, Latin America & Europe
Tuttle Publishing
364 Innovation Drive
North Clarendon, VT 05759-9436 U.S.A.
Tel: 1 (802) 773-8930
Fax: 1 (802) 773-6993
info@tuttlepublishing.com
www.tuttlepublishing.com

Asia-Pacific
Berkeley Books Pte. Ltd.
61 Tai Seng Avenue #02-12
Singapore 534167
Tel: (65) 6280-1330
Fax: (65) 6280-6290
inquiries@periplus.com.sg
www.periplus.com

First edition
12 11 10 09 08   10 9 8 7 6 5 4 3 2 1

Printed in Singapore

Contents

Introduction

Ciao e Benvenuti!   Hi and Welcome!

So…you are dying to finally learn Italian for this upcoming trip to the **Belpaese**, or—no, no—it is because you truly love opera and you absolutely need to understand *Il Dongiovanni*. Or actually, to be fully honest, it's because of the beautiful brown eyes of that charming all-Italian woman you just met, or—in fact—because your **nonna** (grandmother) used to call you "**Tesoro**" and you now want to truly honor her memory and your roots. Or it is simply because you love art, and quality, and architecture; poetry and beauty; and by learning Italian you know you are going to get, in some real way, all that. Plus of course good food and even better wine!

Bene (well…), the good news is that you, with this book, are indeed going to be "making out in Italian" and all that comes with it. As far as the lady or the gentleman with the brown eyes and charming accent…well, that's up to you…but this book will give you some useful tools.

ITALIAN IS EASY…AND YOU ALREADY KNOW IT
Indeed the good news is that speaking Italian—at least, speaking enough to make out—is not as difficult as you have imagined, and you already know more words in Italian than you might believe.

The first easy part about learning Italian is the pronunciation: Italian (unlike English!) is a phonetic language, which means that it's spoken the way that it's written. Letters are pronounced consistently; for each letter there is a corresponding sound. This means that spelling surprises are rare, and most important, that to say something in Italian is pretty straightforward.

The second easy part is that, if speaking a foreign language is about making yourself understood and understanding another person's messages to you—in a word, communicating—Italian is the best bet. Why? Because in Italy you communicate not only with words and sentences (which you'll learn here) but also with your whole body. In an Italian dialogue everything is involved, used, embraced: hands, gestures, facial expressions, sounds. And if you throw yourself into this lively way of communicating, Italians are going to be so fully attuned to you that they'll undoubtedly understand you.

The third easy part is that many many Italian and English words are very similar, or sometimes even identical. That's because they share a common source: Latin. When words have the same root and so are written or pronounced similarly in two languages they are called cognates, and here are some examples of cognates—the Italian you already know:

restaurant	**ristorante**
bank	**banca**
victory	**vittoria**
airport	**aeroporto**
ideal	**ideale**
air conditioning	**l'aria condizionata**

One warning: be mindful of the so-called "false friends," words that look very similar in their Italian/English spellings but that actually have very different meanings. For example, parents and **parenti** (in Italian **parenti** means not "parents" but *all* kinds of family members: "relatives" in English). Or, morbid and **morbido**: **morbido** in Italian means "soft," nothing to do with the English meaning of morbid.

Back to yet another side of the easy part—the non-cognates but universally known words: **amore, pizza, buongiorno, sì, grazie, spaghetti, lasagna, pasta, pesto, vino, ciao...la dolce vita!**

And if you still have any lingering concerns about how easy it will be for you to make out in Italian, just remember that Italian has—especially in recent years—acquired so many English words that the language will sound very familiar. In Italy you'll see and hear "**la privacy,**" "**il check-in,**" "**il computer,**" "**un week-end,**" "**sexy,**" "**un must,**" "**e-mail,**" "**hard-disk,**" "**OK,**" and the list goes on.

A ROMANCE LANGUAGE, A "SEXY" LANGUAGE

Italian is a **lingua romanza** (a Romance language). Like other Romance languages (French, Spanish, Portuguese and Romanian) it derives from Latin, and from Latin it has inherited a series of specific grammar "rules" that makes it at a certain level more articulate and complex than English.

Italian is a very "sexy" language, in that it's extremely focused on gender differences: in fact Italian nouns—all of them aside from the "neutral" ones—have a gender. They are either masculine or feminine, and as a consequence, any words that *describe* a noun, like adjectives and articles, must match its gender.

Gender also comes into play when making plurals, which of course you'll need to do at some point while you're getting along in Italian. Italian does not create the plurals of words by adding an "s" as English does. Instead, Italian changes the last letter of a noun or adjective to create the plural. In the end, all this gender-matching is one of the trickiest parts to learn and remember for foreigners.

Take it as social game—hmm, what's the gender of intelligence?—and you'll start to better understand all the "soft power" of women in Italy...of course **intelligenza** is feminine!

And there are so many other uniquely charming, rather than challenging, aspects of Italian: for example, Italian is a musical-sounding language which for centuries has made it very apt for opera or for very sentimental pop songs. This "genetic" musicality stems from among other things the fact that most Italian words end in a vowel sound, and this creates a very clear rhythm in the flow of a sentence. Speak, speak and you'll find yourself almost singing....

A word about dialects. Italian derives originally from Latin but specifically from the dialects that over the centuries arose from it: Italian is an evolution of what was judged to be the "best" dialect ("lingua volgare")—the Florentine that was spoken and written in the 13th and 14th century.

However, still today, many many different dialects are spoken in different areas of the peninsula. You are not going to recognize the differences initially, although you might notice the diverse accents. Just be aware that if suddenly one day, while in Italy, you find yourself not understanding Italian anymore, you are probably just listening to someone speaking a dialect.

ITALIAN GREETINGS: FORMAL AND INFORMAL

In Italy the ways of greeting someone are several, and they're clearly defined in their use according to the occasions, and the level of familiarity or formality.

Ciao and **Salve** are the equivalents of Hi and Hello. **Salve** means literally "salute" (good health). These two greetings are used informally, with a cheerful, friendly sense. They are common expressions among family and friends, but also with less intimate acquaintances with whom there is a good chemistry and you want to show it.

Buongiorno (Good morning), **Buonasera** (Good evening) are good greetings for strangers, acquaintances and whomever you want to treat with a certain degree of cordial formality.

A presto means "See you soon" and it is also widely used.

Arrivederci is a wonderful little "farewell" Italian word, meaning literally "See each other again." It's a way of parting that assumes you will see each other again and probably soon. It is cheerful and does not have any of the dramatic tone of **addio**.

Addio is the Italian "Farewell" meant as...maybe we won't see each other again. Everything is uncertain with the word **addio**. It was the expression used by the emigrants to say goodbye to their families when they were leaving the **"Bella Italia"** to go to America, the land of opportunity.

When it comes to the *non*-verbal greetings to others, there are interesting peculiarities about the Italian way. First of all, when two friends, not necessarily even close friends, meet they kiss each other on the cheeks: one light kiss on each cheek, not on just one cheek as Americans do. Italians also hug each other but less strongly and with less patting than the American norm.

The handshake exchanged among acquaintances, or colleagues, or dignitaries is also different: Italians shake hands lightly and with only one short up-down movement.

FORMAL AND INFORMAL CONVERSATIONS...
"PUOI DARMI DEL TU"

This is one of the most distinct differences between English and Italian. While English always uses the pronoun "you" when addressing another person or persons, in Italy there is a very specific differentiation depending on your level of intimacy with the person you are talking to and the level of respect you want to show.

The informal way to address people is with the pronoun **tu**, which is used with family, friends, pets, always among students, young people, and often colleagues. The formal way to address people is instead with the pronoun Lei, which is used with persons you've just met, acquaintances, your boss, strangers, dignitaries, and store clerks.

The difficult part of this differentiation for non-natives is not the concept by itself—easy to grasp—but the fact that the other parts of your sentence, like verb forms, possessives, and so on, have to *agree* in their conjugation with the **tu** or the **Lei**. And Italian verbs' conjugations can be, with all their irregular forms, pretty complicated.

In this book, devoted to the goal of "making out in Italian" in an everyday, clear and direct way, we have chosen to use the informal approach. The sentences provided, aside from very few exceptions, use the informal **tu**.

Be assured: Italians will understand you perfectly and they will probably volunteer—you being a foreigner—the following sentence: "**Puoi darmi del tu.**" (You can use the "**tu**" with me.)

On your side you can politely ask: "**Posso darle del tu?**" (Can I use the "**tu**"?)

ASKING QUESTIONS

To pose questions, Italians do not have any equivalent of the "do/does" sort of word arrangement used in English. They simply use the tone of their voice, along with gestures and facial expressions. The context of the sentence will tell you very clearly if a sentence is declarative or interrogative.

Hai parenti in America. (You have relatives in America.)
Hai parenti in America? (Do you have relatives in America?)

Sei felice! (You are happy.)
Sei felice? (Are you happy?)

ALPHABET AND PRONUNCIATION: SOME TRICKS AND TIPS

The Italian alphabet consists of 21 letters plus another 5 letters present only in foreign words. These are the Italian letters:

a b c d e f g h i l m n o p q r s t u v z

These are the foreign ones: j k w x y

Italian pronunciation is pretty easy compared with English, since Italian is spoken the way it is written, but there are some rules.

Consonants, and Combinations

Here some "tricky" pronunciations to keep in mind:

C   When it is before the vowels **i** and **e**, it has to be pronounced like the "ch" in *church*. Examples: **città** (city), **circo** (circus), **centro** (center). But otherwise, it has a sound like "k" (as in "*card*"). Examples: **casa** (home), **conto** (bill).

G   Must be pronounced like the "j" in "*jelly*" when it is before the vowels **i** and **e**. Example: **giardino** (garden). But otherwise, it is pronounced like the "g" of "*gate*." Examples: **galleria** (gallery), **gara** (contest).

GL This is a bit unfamiliar at first for many foreigners who don't have this sound in their own language, but it's not difficult. The **gl** present in Italian words like "**meglio**" (better) is pronounced in a similar way to the "lli" in the English word "mi*lli*on."

H   The **h** in Italian is always silent, no aspiration, not a sound, just a mute presence…think of the pronunciation of "h" in "Ah."

QU Pronounced as in "*quick*."

SC When it is before the vowels **i** and **e**, it is pronounced as "sh." Example: "**scena**" (scene). But otherwise, it has a sound like the "sk" in "*sk*eleton." Example: **brusco** (rude / brisk).

R   This is a tough one. Italian rolls the **r** powerfully, as in *rrrrr*. Just do your best.

The "double" risk

Every Italian consonant—except the **h**—can be doubled. It is very important to stress the double when you speak, since otherwise the sense of the word can be altered: **sette** means seven, while **sete** means thirst. Americans should be particularly attentive when doubling the **tt** to not make a "d" sound. Pronounce both t's using the softness of the "t" in the English word "table."

Vowels

Of the five vowels, three—**a, i, u**—are always pronounced in the same way. Two—**e, o**—can be pronounced with either a short or a long sound.

A   "ah" as in "f*a*ther". Example: **casa** (house)

I   "ee" as in "mar*i*ne". Example: **vino** (wine)

U   "oo" as in "r*u*de". Example: **luna** (moon)

E   Long sound "ay", as in "l*a*te". Example: **sete** (thirst)
    Short sound "eh", as in "l*e*ss". Example: **bello** (beautiful)

O Long sound "oh", as in "most". Example: **sole** (sun)
Short sound "o", as in "cost". Example: **modo** (way)

Also, vowels in Italian are always clearly pronounced, never "skipped" like the silent vowels that exist at the end of many English words. Thus, the word **sole** (sun) is pronounced "*SOH-lay*". Contrast that to the English word for the bottom of a shoe!

Where to Put the Stress
Most words in Italian are pronounced with the stress on the next-to-last syllable. Think about how the word **parola** is said, for instance: *pah-ROH-lah*.

There are some words that are stressed on their last syllable, instead. Those always have an accent mark written on their final vowel, so if you are reading a word, it will be easy for you to notice and you'll know to pronounce it correctly, as in **Così così** (so-so), pronounced *koh-ZEE koh-ZEE*.

There are some words that have their stresses on irregular syllables; you will learn these as you go. And remember, even if you stress a word on the wrong syllable, Italians will still understand you.

One more note about accent marks: sometimes an accent mark is used on a word of just one syllable. Many times this happens when there are two words that sound alike but have different meanings, like **la** (the) and **là** (there).

AVOIDABLE LITTLE MISTAKES
If you want to make a great impression on your new Italian friends, pronounce the following words correctly; these are usually mispronounced by English speakers.

Pinot Grigio: Always avoid pronouncing the **i** that comes after the **g** in the combinations "**gia**," "**gio**," "**giu**." The famous Italian wine Pinot Grigio should be pronounced *GREE-jyoh* (not *gree-jee-oh*); same thing for the name Giovanni (*jyoh-VAHN-nee*).

Bruschetta: The "sch" should not be pronounced as "sh." Avoid the common American mispronunciation of this word; say "sk" for the correct pronunciation, *broo-SKEHT-tah*.

Prosciutto: In this case, the "sciu" must sound like "shoo": *proh-SHOOT-toh*. Do *not* say *proh-skee-oo-toh*!

Spaghetti: Please, please, please: the double "**tt**" has a dou-bled sound, even though it's soft, so say both **t**'s. And avoid like the plague the "**d**" sound of *spah-geh-dee*.

A simplified phonetic transcription system is used throughout the book to help remind you of the correct Italian pronunciations. Read as if it were English, and your "imitated" Italian will be close enough to make out.

And now, **buona fortuna** (good luck) to you. Or better, "**In bocca al lupo**" ("in the mouth of the wolf"), which is an Italian proverb wishing the very best to someone who's launched toward a new enterprise.

You will be pleasantly surprised: learning to "make out in Italian" will be a truly unforgettable journey toward your own **dolce vita**.

Hi...Nice to Meet You
Ciao...Piacere   **1**

Hello! Hi!

Ciao
chah-oh

Buongiorno
bwohn-JYOHR-noh
(do not pronounce the *i*)

Buonasera
bwohn-ah-SEH-rah

Ciao, the cheerful way of greeting people in Italy, is universally used. It's used morning, evening, afternoon and night. It is used to say hello and to say goodbye. It is used when you are intimate with someone or between simple acquaintances, and even in casual encounters on the street, at the bar or at the beach. Sometimes **ciao** is used on purpose to "create" an immediate sense of familiarity, friendship and closeness.

In business situations, in formal occasions or when talking to public officials instead it is important to use the more formal and polite expressions: **buongiorno** for good morning, **buonasera** for good evening. Even when at a store buying something or at a restaurant talking to a waiter/waitress or at the hotel talking to the front desk people, try to use the more formal expression as a sign of respect for the clerks.

What's your name?   **Come ti chiami?**
KOH-meh tee KYAH-mee?

Come ti chiami literally means "How do you call yourself" and it is the way Italians approach people whom they do not know but with whom they want to start talking. That's the way you can be approached everywhere in Italy—at the airport as often as in a coffee shop, or in line in a store or at the post office—and it has to be considered a friendly conversation-starter.

If you like it, use it with no second thought: what in the U.S. might be considered a bit out of line or even invasive, in Italy is the norm. Keep in mind that Italians are naturally communicative (of course there are the "stiff" ones but they are the exception) and they do not find it at all impolite or intrusive to speak to strangers; it is very normal that they will strike up a conversation with you, asking a lot of questions and at the same time providing you with a lot of information about their own life.

My name is Giulia.   **Mi chiamo Giulia.**
mee KYAH-moh Giulia.

Nice to meet you, Giulia!   **Piacere, Giulia! /**
È un piacere!
pyah-CHEH-reh… /
eh oon pyah-CHEH-reh.

Think the word **piacere** (literally "pleasure") all the time. It is your door-opener in Italy: try to always say it when you meet or you are introduced to someone for the first time, be it the person who greets you at the hotel and tells you his/her name, or a friend or a friend of a friend, or a business partner, or a lovely woman/man you just met. Say **piacere** as the Italians do: shaking hands (only once, with one up-down shake), smiling and looking straight in the eyes of the other person. You can also say **È un piacere**: "It is (indeed) a pleasure." Never forget that "pleasure" is a key component of the Italian soul and lifestyle.

Guess what it is.	**Indovina!** *een-doh-VEE-nah!*
What did you say?	**Cosa hai detto?** *KOH-zah ah-ee DEHT-toh?* (do not pronounce the *h*)
Where do you live?	**Dove abiti?** *DOH-vay ah-BEE-tee?*

Dove (where), **cosa** (what), **come** (how), **quando** (when), **quanto** (how much), **perche** (why), **chi** (who): are all important expressions in the Italian language, used to introduce a question.

Where do you come from?	**Da dove vieni?** *dah DOH-veh VYEH-nee?*
How old are you?	**Quanti anni hai?** *KWAHN-tee AHN-nee ah-ee?*
Are you a student?	**Studi o lavori?** *STOO-dee oh* *lah-VOH-ree?*

The literal translation is "do you study or do you work?", and this is the way you'd most often phrase this question in Italy, not knowing what the other person does.

Where are you studying?	**Dove studi?**
	DOH-veh STOO-dee?

What's your job?   **Che lavoro fai?**
kay lah-VOH-roh fah-ee?

Do you come here often?   **Vieni qui spesso?**
VYEH-nee kwee SPEHS-soh?

Have I seen you before?   **Ti ho mai visto prima?**
tee oh mah-ee VEE-stoh
PREE-mah?

Ti is the equivalent of you. (Depending on what part it plays in the grammar of a sentence, "you" has all these forms in Italian: **tu; te; ti.**)

The following expressions are used between people who already know each other.

Haven't seen you   **Quanto tempo! / È un po'**
    around for while!   **che non ci vediamo!**
KWAHN-toh TEHM-poh! / eh
oon poh kay nohn chee veh
DYAH-moh!

Quanto tempo, the most common of these two colloquial expressions, can be used when you see someone unexpectedly, but also when you meet someone at a scheduled appointment, if it's a while since you've seen that person. It means literally "How much time…!"

È un po' che non ci vediamo, literally "It is a while that we do not see each other," can be used in every occasion, just like the previous expression; however it conveys less of an exclamation connotation.

How are you?	**Come stai?** *KOH-meh stah-ee?*
How is it going?	**Come va?** *KOH-meh vah?*
Nice to see you again.	**Che piacere rivederti.** *kay pyah-CHEH-reh ree-veh-DEHR-tee.*

It means literally "What a pleasure to see you again" and it's a phrase you will hear—and probably say—very often.

What's up?	**Come va? / Quali novità?** *KOH-may vah? / KWAH-lee noh-vee-TAH?*

Come va? is extremely common in everyday conversation. It's a friendly expression whose meanings include how's it going?, how have you been doing?, what's new?

It is used when you see someone again after a while apart, and it's also used just as often to greet someone with whom you are in touch continuously, perhaps a colleague you see at work every morning, or a friend, or a spouse when you return home after a workday.

Quali novità? means literally "is there news." It can be used interchangeably with **Come va?**

What's happening?	**Cosa succede?** *KOH-zah soo-KSEH-deh?*
Nothing much!	**Niente di che!** *NYEHN-teh dee chay!*

This colloquial phrase can come in very handy for you, anytime you want to answer a generic question without going into details, or as way let a conversation die: lit. "nothing of something."

Nothing special. **Niente di speciale.**
NYEHN-teh dee speh-see-AH-lay.

Okay, I guess. **Bene, credo.**
BEH-neh, KRAY-doh.

I'm fine. **Sto bene.**
stoh BEH-neh.

So-so / Not good, not bad. **Così così / nè bene nè male.**
koh-ZEE koh-ZEE / neh
BEH-neh neh MAH-leh.

Così così is a very common expression used in many circumstances to reply in a neutral way to the question about how you are doing. It can have a more negative or more positive connotation, according to the tone of voice used or other non-verbal cues.

I wanted to see you / **Volevo vederti /**
   I missed you. **Mi mancavi.**
voh-LEH-voh veh-DEHR-tee /
mee mahn-KAH-vee.

How have you been doing? **Come sei stato/a?**
KOH-meh seh-ee STAH-toh/tah?

What have you been doing? **Cosa hai fatto?**
KOH-zah ah-ee FAHT-toh?

What's wrong?	**Qualcosa non va?** *kwahl-KOH-zah nohn vah?*
I'm really busy (with work / university)	**Sono molto impegnato/a con il lavoro / l'università.** *SOH-noh MOHL-toh eem-peh-NYAH-toh/tah kohn eel lah-VOH-roh / loo-nee-vehr-see-TAH.*
I'm not feeling well.	**Non mi sento bene.** *nohn mee SEHN-toh BEH-neh.*
I've got a cold.	**Ho preso un raffreddore.** *oh PREH-zoh oon rahf-frehd-DOH-reh.*
I'm a bit depressed.	**Sono un po' depresso/a.** *SOH-noh oon poh deh-PREHS-soh/sah.*
I'm tired.	**Sono stanco/a.** *SOH-noh STAHN-koh/kah.*
I'm sleepy.	**Ho sonno.** *oh SOHN-noh.*

Notice that in Italian the verb used for this expression is "to have" (**avere**), not "to be" (**essere**): Italians "own" a feeling of being sleepy, as they own many other conditions and feelings...**Ho fame** (I am hungry, lit. "I have hunger") or **Ho sete** (I am thirsty, lit. "I have thirst"); **Ho freddo** (I am cold, lit. "I have cold") or **Ho caldo** (I am hot, lit. "I have heat").

I'm not sleepy.	**Non ho sonno.** *nohn oh SOHN-noh.*

I'll be okay / I'll work it out.	**Andrà tutto bene.** *ahn-DRAH TOOT-toh BEH-neh.*
That's a bummer / tough!	**Che pensiero deprimente!** *kay pehn-SYEH-roh* *deh-pree-MEHN-teh!*
That can't be helped / There is nothing you can do about it.	**Non c'è niente da fare /** **Non c'è soluzione.** *nohn cheh NYEHN-teh dah* *FAH-reh / nohn cheh* *soh-loo-TSYOH-nay.*
That's unfortunate / that's a shame.	**Che peccato!** *kay pehk-KAH-toh!*

This is an interesting difference between English and Italian, concerning the words used to express the same concept: English uses the word "shame" which has a social meaning related to the sense of pride and honor; while the Italian language uses the word **peccato** whose meaning is "sin," revealing the profound Catholic roots of its culture.

Cheer up!	**Tirati sù / Stai sù.** *TEE-rah-tee soo / stah-ee soo.*

Learn these two simple expressions (lit. "pull yourself up"; "stay upbeat") which are used all the time, and use them yourself every time you see someone with a sad or simply tired look: you will attract a lot of gratitude!

What's on your mind?	**Cosa stai pensando?** *KOH-zah stah-ee* *pehn-SAHN-doh?*

Literally, "What are you thinking?"

Nothing.	**Niente.**
	NYEHN-teh.

When Italians use **niente** to answer the specific question above (of what's on their mind), it means they have no intention of continuing to talk. It happens at times, even though more often they are open to sharing thoughts, feelings, etc. even in the course of a casual encounter. Both men and women are usually open to discussing almost everything in Italy, and they would not find anything inappropriate about you asking. They take it as a normal nice way of being interested in them.

I was just thinking.	**Stavo solo pensando.**
	STAH-voh SOH-loh
	pehn-SAHN-doh.
Leave me alone.	**Lasciami solo.**
	lah-SHYAH-mee SOH-loh.
It's none of your business.	**Non sono affari tuoi.**
	nohn SOH-noh ah-FAH-ree
	TWOH-ee.
Is Sally okay?	**Sta bene Sally?**
	stah BEH-neh Sally?
How is Sally doing?	**Come sta Sally?**
	KOH-meh stah Sally?
Seen Jeff?	**Hai visto Jeff?**
	ah-ee VEE-stoh Jeff?
I saw / met Kerry.	**Ho visto Kerry.**
	oh VEE-stoh Kerry.

I want to see you soon.

Vediamoci presto!
vee-dyah-MOH-chee PREH-stoh!

In this case, Italians would most likely say "Let's see each other soon."

Goodbye.

Ciao. Addio. Arrivederci.
chah-oh. AHD-dyoh.
ahr-ree-veh-DEHR-chee.

As we discussed (see page 15), **ciao** is okay in most occasions; **addio** is the equivalent of the more formal English "farewell"; **arrivederci** means "see you again." After someone says the sentence **Vediamoci presto,** as on the previous page, the best choice would be either **Ciao** or **Arrivederci.**

Yes, No, Maybe
Sì, No, Forse

2

Yes.   **Sì.**
see.

No.   **No.**
noh.

That's right.   **Esatto / Proprio così.**
eh-ZAH-toh / PROH-pree-oh
koh-ZEE.

Both of these expressions are commonly used.

I think so.   **Penso di sì.**
PEHN-soh dee see.

I agree.   **Sono d'accordo.**
SOH-noh dahk-KOHR-doh.

So am I / Me too.   **Anche io.**
AHN-keh ee-oh.

I see / I got it / I understand.   **Capisco.**
kah-PEE-skoh.

All right, that's okay.   **Va bene.**
vah BEH-neh.

No problem.	**Non c'è problema.** *nohn chay proh-BLEH-mah.*
Really?	**Davvero?** *dahv-VEH-roh?*
Is that so?	**È vero?** *eh VEH-roh?*

In Italian, questions are not introduced by phrasings like "do you / did you," etc. The only way to know if someone is asking you something, or to ask a question yourself, is with the tone of voice and non-verbal cues. Do not worry, you will catch on to it quickly!

Yeah, I know.	**Sì, lo so.** *see, loh soh.*
I guess so.	**Credo di sì.** *KRAY-doh dee see.*
It might be true.	**Può essere vero.** *pwoh ehs-SEH-reh VEH-roh.*
Maybe.	**Forse / Può essere.** *FOHR-seh / pwoh ehs-SEH-reh.*

Either expression can be used; you will hear both of them frequently in your travels.

Maybe not.	**Forse no.** *FOHR-seh noh.*
Because…	**Perchè…** *pehr-KAY…*

The Italian language has only one word to say "because" and "why": **perchè**.

That's not right.

Non va bene. / Non è giusto.
nohn vah BEH-neh. /
nohn eh JYOO-stoh.

I wonder.

Mi chiedo.
mee KYEH-doh.

I don't think so / I doubt it.

Credo di no / Dubito.
KRAY-doh dee noh. /
DOO-bee-toh.

I'm not sure.

Non sono sicuro/a.
nohn SOH-noh
see-KOO-roh/rah.

There is no way of knowing.

Non c'è modo di saperlo.
nohn chay MOH-doh dee
sah-PEHR-loh.

I can't say for sure.

Non sono sicuro/a.
nohn SOH-noh
see-KOO-roh/rah.

But...

Ma...
mah...

How come?

Come mai?
KOH-meh mah-ee?

What's the difference?	**Che differenza c'è?**
	keh deef-feh-REHN-tsah chay?

What do you mean?	**Cosa vuoi dire?**
	KOH-zah vwoy DEE-reh?

The real meaning of this question can be interpreted only through the posture and the general attitude of the person posing it: Italians can ask **Cosa vuoi dire?** in a very innocent way, but the same expression can also easily be used to provoke an argument, opening doubts on the true significance and purpose of what has just been said.

Is something wrong?	**Qualcosa non va?**
	kwahl-KOH-zah nohn vah?

Why not?	**Perchè no?**
	pehr-KAY noh?

Are you serious?	**Sul serio? / Seriamente?**
	sool SEH-ryoh? /
	seh-ryah-MEHN-teh?

Are you sure?	**Sei sicuro/a?**
	seh-ee see-KOO-roh/rah?

You don't mean it? /	**Scherzi o dici sul serio?**
You are joking?	*SKEHR-tsee oh DEE-chee sool*
	SEH-ryoh?

This is a very common expression used in a variety of occasions, mainly colloquial, to ask someone if he/she is joking or very seriously standing behind his/her thoughts or positions on a specific issue. It can be generally interpreted in a neutral way. But if used in more formal talks, like at work, with your boss, or even in an everyday business transaction, this expression can be interpreted as a provocation or the beginning of an argument since you are casting doubts on the other person's sincerity or real intentions.

Absolutely.	**Assolutamente.** *ahs-soh-LOO-tah-MEHN-teh.*
Definitely.	**Senza dubbio.** *SEHN-tsah DOOB-byoh.*

Literally, "Without a doubt."

Of course.	**Certo / Naturale.** *CHEHR-toh / nah-too-RAH-leh.*
You better believe it!	**Fai meglio a crederci!** *fah-ee MEH-lyoh ah* *kreh-DEHR-chee.*

Note that the **gl** sound in **meglio** (better) does not exist in English pronunciation. To make this sound, pronounce the **gl** like the **lli** in "million."

There it is.	**Ecco. Eccolo / la / li / le.** *EHK-koh. EHK-koh-loh /* *lah / lee / leh.*

Ecco is a good word to know and to learn to use in a versatile way just as the Italians do. It can be used when you present or show something: a job project just finished, a cake just baked, a gift, a person, an object. You can use the expression **Eccomi** to introduce your own arrival at an appointment. You can add one of the endings, **lo / la / li / le**— **eccolo, eccola, eccoli, eccole:** here he is / she is / they (masc.) are / they (fem.) are—when you want to introduce an object or a person.

That was good. **È stato bello.**
eh STAH-toh BEHL-loh.

The Italian language uses **bello** (beautiful) instead of **buono** (good) to express a very pleasant experience: a vacation, a book just read, a trip, an afternoon spent together.... This isn't surprising considering the sense of aesthetic beauty that characterizes Italian culture in all its expressions, including the linguistic one.

Right on / Great! **Perfetto / Bene! / Bravo!**
pehr-FEHT-toh / BEH-neh! / BRAH-voh!

Although "great" is used very often in casual English, the Italian language uses the word **perfetto** or the word **bene** which means "good/well": again the Italian culture's sense of aesthetics is prevalent in the word choices. **Perfetto** refers to the ideal of perfect harmony. In fact, in Italian, you would almost never use the literal Italian equivalent of "great" (the word **grande**) unless in a sort of teasing, childlike way. An athlete's performance, a soccer game, could *possibly* be **grande**...but most often you'd simply say **Bravo**!

You're kidding me. **Mi prendi in giro.**
mee PREHN-dee een JEE-roh.

Try to remember this beautiful idomatic expression whose literal meaning is "you are taking me around in circles." It is used abundantly, most of the time while smiling and in a very friendly way. Occasionally it can be used in an argument.

This is too good to be true. **È troppo bello per essere vero.**
eh TROHP-poh BEHL-loh pehr ehs-SEH-reh VEH-roh.

That's wrong.	**È sbagliato.** *eh sbah-LYAH-toh.*
No way / Stop joking.	**No, non scherzare.** *noh, nohn skehr-TSAH-reh.*
That's impossible.	**È impossibile.** *eh eem-pohs-see-BEE-leh.*
Forget it!	**Scordatelo!** *skohr-dah-TEH-loh.*
Bullshit!	**Balle / Palle! / Stupidaggini!** *BAHL-leh / PAHL-leh! /* *STOO-pee-dah-DJEE-nee!*

The first two words (**balle** or **palle** are actually the same word—the first consonant can change without affecting its meaning) are used in colloquial everyday language, referring to men's testicles. Italians say **Balle** (or **Palle**) when someone says things almost impossible to believe. But if you want to "translate" the American term "bullshit" in a less rude and more polite way you can say **Stupidaggini**, which is the equivalent of "silly things."

I don't care (anything's fine).	**Non importa.** *nohn eem-POHR-tah.* *(vah BEH-neh TOOT-toh.)*

It means nothing to me.

Non ha importanza per me.
*nohn ah eem-pohr-TAHN-
tsah pehr meh.*

I am not interested.

**Non sono interessato /
non mi interessa.**
*nohn SOH-noh een-teh-rehs-
SAH-toh / nohn mee
een-teh-REHS-sah.*

These two expressions can be used interchangeably.

Now? Later? When?
Adesso? Dopo? Quando? 3

Got a second / minute?	**Hai un attimo / minuto?** *ah-ee oon AHT-tee-moh /* *mee-NOO-toh?*

In Italy it's very common to use either of these two phrases in everyday language.

Till when?	**Fino a quando?** *fee-noh ah KWAHN-doh?*
When?	**Quando?** *KWAHN-doh?*
About what time?	**Più o meno a che ora?** *pyoo oh MEH-noh ah kay* *OH-rah?*

This expression reflects a common Italian approach to life; that's why Italians use it extremely frequently. **Più o meno**—meaning "more or less"—is used in many different occasions, not all related to time: it's used for weights (if you are shopping for produce for example), locations, feelings, choices to make, time of departure, time of an appointment, and so on.

Italian "imprecision" is in some aspects a stereotype, but it is also rooted in an attitude, a way of being. It can be seen as a creative trait that leaves room for flexibility, relaxation and...the good life.

Just think: Italian does not have a word for "schedule."
What does this say?

Clearly there are plenty of exceptions and consequent-
ly there are very precise and detail-oriented Italians. Indeed
the artistic accomplishments that have made Italy famous,
or the success of many industries from fashion to cuisine to
automotive design, show that in Italy there also exists an
extreme attention to detail.

Is it too early?	**È troppo presto?** *eh TROHP-poh PREH-stoh?*
Is it too late?	**È troppo tardi?** *eh TROHP-poh TAHR-dee?*
When is convenient for you?	**Quando va bene per te?** *KWAHN-doh vah BEH-neh* *pehr teh?*
How about the 18th?	**Il 18? / Va bene il 18?** *eel dee-chee-OHT-toh? /* *vah BEH-neh eel* *dee-chee-OHT-toh?*

To ask a followup question with a precise date or time for
an appointment, Italians often use only the date ac-
companied by the determinative article (the article **il** is
used for all the numbers) without adding any other words:
"The 18th?" In other occasions, they say **Va bene il**... (Is it
okay, the...). You can choose either phrasing.

Then when can you make it?	**Quando puoi esserci?** *KWAHN-doh pwoy* *ehs-SEHR-chee?*

What time can I come over?	**A che ora posso passare?**
	ah kay OH-rah POHS-soh
	pahs-SAH-reh?

A che ora is the exact equivalent of "at what time," and it is an important little expression to learn considering its wide use for a traveller.

What time do we leave?	**A che ora partiamo?**
	ah kay OH-rah
	pahr-TYAH-moh?

What time do we arrive?	**A che ora arriviamo?**
	ah kay OH-rah
	ahr-ree-VYAH-moh?

Punctuality is often not a characteristic of Italian personal and social life—not in the mail system, not in trans-portation, not even in the television schedule. It is a fact of everyday life that Italians are used to: just go prepared. Taking that same attitude, and viewing the Italian lack of punctuality as an easygoing part of your visit to a sunny and cheerful country, will help you have a successful visit.

Here are some examples of how to navigate the Italian "code" of social life with an eye to punctuality or the lack of it.

If you are invited to dinner **più o meno alle 8 p.m.** (more or less at 8 p.m.), it is almost impolite to present yourself at the door exactly at 8 p.m.; it is unthinkable to arrive earlier (you would find your hosts probably in total disarray, frenetically organizing last-minute things and look-ing at you in dismay). What you need to respect is the unspoken rule of the 15-minute delay: you should arrive 15 minutes later then the invitation time and you will be con-sidered a perfect gentleman or a perfect lady. Generally it is considered good form to arrive between 10 and 15 minutes late, and it is acceptable to arrive between 20 and 30 minutes late, but any further delay would require a phone call.

Of course the situation is slightly different if you have a date or a meeting that's taking place on the street, in front of a movie theater or in a coffee shop; but still the 10-to-15-minute delay is considered very normal.

Many times, unfortunately, you will find the same tendency to an imprecise schedule in the departure and arrival times of trains and buses. Things have definitely improved in recent years, though; for example, Italian authorities have imposed penalty payments on the railroad system to compensate passengers if trains are delayed more than 30 minutes. But if this happens to you, keep in mind that to file for reimbursement you will be in a very long, slow line; and the payback will arrive…probably late.

Are you ready?	**Sei pronto/a? / Sono pronti/e?** (for the plural "you") *seh-ee PROHN-toh/tah? / SOH-noh PROHN-tee-/teh?*
When will you do it?	**Quando lo farai?** *KWAHN-doh loh FAH-rah-ee?*
How long will it take?	**Quanto tempo ti occorrerà?** *KWAHN-toh TEHM-poh tee ohk-kohr-REH-rah?*
Next time.	**La prossima volta.** *lah PROHS-see-mah VOHL-tah.*
Maybe later.	**Forse dopo.** *FOHR-seh DOH-poh.*

Later. **Dopo / più tardi.**
DOH-poh / pyoo TAHR-dee.

Soon. **Presto.**
PREH-stoh.

Not yet. **Non ancora.**
nohn ahn-KOH-rah.

The same word, **ancora**, is used in Italian for both "yet" and "still."

Not now. **Non adesso.**
nohn ah-DEHS-soh.

The last time. **L'ultima volta.**
LOOL-tee-mah VOHL-tah.

I don't know when. **Non so quando.**
nohn soh KWAHN-doh.

I don't know now. **Non lo so adesso.**
nohn loh soh ah-DEHS-soh.

I don't know yet. **Non lo so ancora.**
nohn loh soh ahn-KOH-rah.

Someday. **Un giorno.**
oon JYOOR-noh.

Always. **Sempre.**
SEHM-preh.

Not next time. **Non la prossima volta.**
nohn lah PROHS-see-mah
      VOHL-tah.

| Anytime is fine. | **In ogni momento va bene.**
een OH-nyee moh-MEHN-toh
vah BEH-neh. |

The **gn** in **ogni** (every) is pronounced like the **ni** in the English word "onion."

| You decide when. | **Decidi tu quando.**
deh-CHEE-dee too KWAHN-doh. |

| That's a bad day for me. | **Non è un giorno buono per**
me.
nohn eh oon JYOOR-noh
BWOH-noh pehr meh. |

| That day is fine. | **Quel giorno va bene.**
kwehl JYOOR-noh vah
BEH-neh. |

| Let's begin! | **Cominciamo!**
koh-meen-CHYAH-moh! |

| It will take only a minute. | **Basta un minuto.**
BAH-stah oon mee-NOO-toh. |

Basta is a key word in Italian. It has two main meanings. In this case **basta** indicates "to be sufficient, to be enough." The expression **basta così** means "it's enough."

But **basta** also means "stop": it is used to order some-one to stop doing something annoying (noises, etc.), as in **Basta giocare** ("Stop playing," to kids), **Basta gridare** ("Stop screaming").

Let's continue.	**Continuiamo.** *kohn-tee-nyoo-ee-YAH-moh.*
Do it later.	**Fallo dopo.** *FAHL-loh DOH-poh.*
I'll be finished soon.	**Finirò presto.** *fee-nee-ROH PREHS-toh.*
I've finished.	**Ho finito.** *oh fee-NEE-toh.*
Finished?	**Finito?** *fee-NEE-toh?*
Finished already?	**Già finito?** *jyah fee-NEE-toh?*

Let's Go Out!
Usciamo!

4

Shall we go and see it?

Andiamo a vedere...?
*ahn-DYAH-moh ah
veh-DEH-reh...?*

This is the phrase used when someone proposes a trip to the movie theater, to a theatre or to a concert. All are common activities in Italy: Italians still love to go to see a movie despite the obvious availability of films on tapes or on DVD for home viewing. Big cities like Rome and Milan enjoy the premiers of the newest movies, and you will see long lines snaking outside theaters that offer new releases. But in smaller towns too, movies remain a popular attraction. **Andiamo a vedere** is also used all the time to invite someone to go and see a monument, a square or a natural attraction: a landscape of particular beauty, a sunset (**tramonto**), the sunrise (**alba**), the sea (**il mare**), the stars (**le stelle**) and so on.

Be prepared for this phrase, because if you're ever asked out for a date or just for a friendly appointment—in Rome, say—you may receive a similar proposal: "**Andiamo a vedere il tramonto a Piazza di Spagna.**" ("Let's go and see the sunset from the Spanish Steps.")...

Did you see it?

Lo hai visto?
loh ah-ee VEE-stoh?

I saw it.

Lo ho visto.
loh oh VEE-stoh.

I didn't see it.	**Non lo ho visto.** *nohn loh oh VEE-stoh.*
I couldn't see it.	**Non sono riuscito a vederlo.** *non SOH-noh ryoo-SEE-toh ah* *veh-DEHR-loh.*
I don't want to see it.	**Non voglio vederlo.** *non VOH-lyoh veh-DEHR-loh.*
Do you want to see…?	**Vuoi vedere…?** *vwoy veh-DEH-reh…?*
Shall we get a video or a DVD or watch TV instead?	**Prendiamo un divudi o una cassetta o guardiamo la tivù?** *prehn-DYAH-moh oon dee-voo-DEE oh oo-nah kahs-SEHT-tah oh gwahr-DYAH-moh lah tee-VOO?*

Yes: Italians still use the VCR a lot, the DVD player is not nearly as common as it is in the United States, and TV channels are still the favorite home entertainment.

Look.	**Guarda.** *GWAHR-dah.*

Look at this!   **Guarda questo / Guarda qui!**
                                 GWAHR-dah KWEH-stoh /
                                 GWAHR-dah kwee!

In Italian you use **questo** (this) when there is a specific object to look at, and **qui** (here), when the thing to look at is not being specified. Note, both words refer to something/someone that's very close to the viewer.

Look at that!   **Guarda quello / Guarda là!**
                                 GWAHR-dah KWEHL-loh /
                                 GWAHR-dah LAH!

Here also, Italians may say **quello** (that) when there is a specific object or person pretty far away to observe, and **là** (there) when the distant object is not specified.

Take a look.   **Dai un'occhiata.**
                                 dah-ee oon oh-KYAH-tah.

An idiomatic expression meaning "to give an eye" to something.

Don't look.   **Non guardare.**
                                 nohn GWAHR-dah-reh.

I'll show you.   **Ti faccio vedere.**
                                 tee FAH-chyoh veh-DEH-reh.

I won't show you.   **Non ti faccio vedere.**
                                 nohn tee FAH-chyoh
                                 veh-DEH-reh.

SHOPPING

Shall we go shopping?

**Andiamo a fare spese? /
Andiamo a fare
"shopping"?**
*ahn-DYAH-moh ah FAH-reh
SPEH-zeh? / ahn-DYAH-moh
ah FAH-reh "shopping"?*

A growing number of Italians use the English word "shopping" instead of the idiomatic expression **andare a fare spese**, but the authentic Italian phrasing still is the most often heard. One difference is that Italians almost always specify what kind of shopping they want to do: food shopping, clothing shopping and so on.

Let's go shopping
downtown.

**Andiamo a fare spese in
centro.**
*ahn-DYAH-moh ah FAH-reh
SPEH-zeh een
CHEHN-troh.*

I want to go shopping for
clothes.

**Voglio andare a comprare
dei vestiti.**
*VOH-lyoh ahn-DAH-reh ah
kohm-PRAH-reh deh-ee
veh-STEE-tee.*

Clothes shopping in Italy is serious activity that requires preparation, concentration, and…action. In Italy when people go shopping for clothing, it's generally in the center of town, where the most beautiful shops, designer name stores and boutiques are. Whenever you step into these kinds of stores, **le commesse / i commessi** (shop assistants) usually help you to find the right dress, pants, sizes; they help you to try them on, to coordinate the colors, and so on. You are pampered during the whole experience and leave the store feeling infinitely more sophisticated than when you walked in. Both men and women in Italy love to wear—and so to buy—quality and trendy clothes, shoes, ties, purses, and the list goes on. Going to department stores for clothing shopping is less popular in Italy than in the U.S., mainly because there are fewer chains in Italy; the majority of the shops are individually owned and managed.

Another venue for clothes shopping is the outlet stores of famous designers and brands, but these too are much less common than in the U.S. Finally, there is also the local market. In every city and village there is a large weekly or monthly market where it is possible to buy diverse items from food to shoes, from plants and furniture to clothing.

STROLLING

Shall we go in the center / downtown / in the square?

Andiamo in centro / in piazza?
ahn-DYAH-moh een CHEHN-troh / een PYAH-tsah?

This is the most common activity in Italy after work, or after a long day spent studying or just at home, especially in small to medium-sized towns: to go to the central square, which has remained the focal point of civic life for centuries. Gathering in the squares is such a natural, easy form of socialization that Italians keep nurturing and experiencing it day after day. Every village on the Italian peninsula has an ancient square, from the Roman times or the Middle Ages, with adjacent churches, walls or buildings and often a fountain or a statue in the center of the square.

Nowadays Italians, old and young, naturally gather after 5 p.m. in these squares just to chat, to get together, to have an **aperitivo** (a glass of wine before dinner). You normally see not only students, businessmen, and workmen in the

piazza, but stay-at-home moms going around with their strollers or letting the kids playing freely on the ancient cobblestones.

Shall we take a stroll in the center [of town]?	**Andiamo a fare una passeggiata in centro?** *ahn-DYAH-moh ah FAH-reh OO-nah pah-seh-DJYAH-tah een CHEHN-troh?*

You might receive a proposal of this type, to go with someone you have just met to take a stroll in the center. Italians love to walk in crowded areas of their towns just taking it easy and people-watching. What better, easier and more innocent way to start a friendship, or even a... courtship.

Shall we go for a coffee / for an ice cream / to a pastry shop?	**Andiamo a prendere un caffè, un gelato, in pasticceria?** *ahn-DYAH-moh ah prehn-DEH-reh oon kahf-FEH, oon jeh-LAH-toh, een pah-stee-cheh-REE-ah?*

Again: this is what Italians do, and so it's what they naturally propose to do to new or old acquaintances, and it's what you will be easily drawn to do while in Italy, the **Belpaese** ("beautiful country"): Going for ice cream in the evening or during lazy summer afternoons; for espresso coffee in lovely, cozy, busy coffee shops; inside a **pasticceria** to eat a sweet and drink a **succo di frutta** (fruit juice). Less often Italians may go for alcohol drinking, especially on a date. But it is common to have a drink in a bar before dinner particularly in the northern, and so colder, regions.

Shall we go for a drink? | **Andiamo a bere qualcosa?**
ahn-DYAH-moh ah BEH-reh kwahl-KOH-zah?

The moment to go out for a drink is, in Italy, usually before dinner when Italians will perhaps offer you a simple glass of wine or wine mixed with water (a drink called **spritz** in the North). After dinner sometimes a liquor is offered. But generally, the habit of drinking in company as a form of entertainment is much less common than in other countries.

Wine, however, is considered and so consumed as a "food" in Italy; and as such, it is drunk mainly with meals. In the northern regions you can often find, along the central streets of towns, places called **osterie**. These are bars where people gather to drink a glass of wine and eat small **panini** or **tartine** (sandwiches). The ritual of going to visit wineries in Tuscany, Trentino, Friuli, Puglia, and other wine-producing regions is also well known and enjoyed.

Shall we go get something? | **Andiamo a prendere qualcosa?**
ahn-DYAH-moh ah prehn-DEH-reh kwahl-KOH-zah?

I wonder where we should go. | **Mi chiedo dove andare.**
mee KYEH-doh DOH-veh ahn-DAH-reh.

I know a good place. | **Conosco un bel posticino.**
koh-NOH-skoh oon behl poh-stee-CHEE-noh.

Shall we go clubbing /
   dancing this Friday /
   Saturday?

**Andiamo in discoteca /
   a ballare questo venerdì /
   sabato?**
*ahn-DYAH-moh een dee-skoh-
   TEH-kah / ah bahl-LAH-reh
   KWEH-stoh veh-nehr-DEE /
   SAH-bah-toh?*

Let's go to your favorite
   club.

**Andiamo nel tuo posto
   preferito.**
*ahn-DYAH-moh nehl too-oh
   POH-stoh preh-feh-REE-toh.*

Talk to Me
Parlami!

5

Talk to me!

Parlami! / Dimmi!
PAHR-lah-mee! / DEEM-mee!

Either of these two verbs can be used.

It's a true cliché: Italians love to talk, to be talked to, to communicate verbally and physically. They are not often in silence. Of course there are the more private personalities, but usually it is impossible, unless in a tense situation, to be in the same room with an Italian and be quiet. Silence most often would indicate uneasiness, or some underlying conflicts. If you could read the Italian mind you would see that for them, unless there is some very pressing worrisome issue in their mind, there is absolutely no reason *not* to chat, comment about the weather, the news of day, etc.

So, to be prepared: you will be asked—directly as with the above sentence or indirectly—to talk, to share your thoughts, projects, feelings of the moment, opinions on everything. And that's also why Italians are so very opinionated about absolutely everything: it is a matter of training, and something practiced since childhood.

Listen.

Ascolta.
ah-SKOHL-tah.

Listen to me!

Ascoltami!
ah-SKOHL-tah-mee!

Don't ask me that.	**Non me lo chiedere.**
	nohn meh loh kyeh-DEH-reh.

Of course even for the very direct, expressive and uninhibited Italians there are some topics that are off limits. Here is the sentence you will hear in these cases, and that you can of course use every time you feel too "invaded" and do not want to talk about something, but remember: pronounce it with a smile and a friendly attitude so that it will be taken not as a cold, aloof or even provocative response, but simply as a request of respect for your privacy.

Did you hear me / him / them?	**Mi hai sentito? / Lo ha hai sentito? / Li hai sentiti?**
	mee ah-ee sehn-TEE-toh? /
	loh ah ah-ee sehn-TEE-toh? /
	lee ah-ee sehn-TEE-toh?

Remember that in Italian not only the personal pronouns change (me/him/them become **mi/lo/li** in the object position) but also the conjugation of the accompanying verb, in this case **sentire**, must agree with the pronoun (singular or plural, masculine or feminine). This is probably the most difficult aspect of the Italian language to master for English speakers. One assurance: Italians will understand you in any case.

I could not hear.	**Non sono riuscito a sentire.**
	nohn SOH-noh ryoo-SEE-toh ah
	sehn-TEE-reh.

I don't want to hear.	**Non voglio ascoltare / sentire.**
	nohn VOH-lyoh ah-skohl-TAH-reh /
	sehn-TEE-reh.

To say **voglio**, pronounce the **gl** like the **lli** in "million."

Speak up.

Parla più forte.
PAHR-lah pyoo FOHR-teh.

Speak more slowly.

Parla più piano. /
Parla lentamente.
PAHR-lah pyoo PYAH-noh. /
PAHR-lah
lehn-tah-MEHN-teh.

You can use either expression.

Say it again.

Ripeti / Puoi ripetere per
favore?
ree-PEH-tee / pwoy
ree-peh-TEH-reh
pehr fah-VOH-reh?

Italians use both of these expressions: the first one is more abrupt, almost an order, to be used only when in a real hurry, and the second one is more polite.

Let's talk in Italian.

Parliamo in Italiano.
pahr-LYAH-moh een
ee-tah-LYAH-noh.

Your Italian is really good.

Parli bene italiano.
PAHR-lee BEH-neh
ee-tah-LYAH-noh.

Be confident: Italians are so unaccustomed to see foreigners trying to speak their language that they will praise your effort.

Let's talk in English.

Parliamo in inglese.
pahr-LYAH-moh een
een-GLEH-seh.

Many Italians know some English, especially from the movie and the music industries. Even people in their seventies know the words of the American pop standards that were popular after World War II or of the evergreens like Frank Sinatra. Nowadays the youth generally study English at least from middle school on, and so if you want to have more chance of being understood in English on the streets of Italy, you should approach a young person. They will generally try their best to respond to you. Many of them go to the United Kingdom in the summer to polish their English; fewer come to the United States. So in the most educated young people you may notice a distinct British accent, and in all the other ones a very pronounced Italian accent but a lot of willingness to try to speak your language.

You are good at English.   **Parli bene l'inglese.**
PAHR-lee BEH-neh
leen-GLEH-seh.

If you compliment Italians to make them speak more to you in English, be assured that they will keep talking to you, and if they do not know the words, they will make up for it with a lot of hand, arm and body gestures. If they are trying to explain to you something very practical, like walking or driving directions, they will probably touch you, make you turn your body to look in the right direction, pat your shoulders and so on; do not be surprised! In Italy you are *not* kept at arm's length! The sense of "personal space" and physical distance/closeness is truly different from the typical American's sense.

Yes, you really are good.   **Sì, sei proprio bravo/a.**
see, seh-ee PROH-pree-oh
BRAH-voh/vah.

Where did you learn English?	**Dove hai imparato l'inglese?** *DOH-veh ah-ee eem-pah-RAH-toh leen-GLEH-seh?*
How long have you been learning English?	**Per quanto tempo hai studiato l'inglese?** *pehr KWAHN-toh TEHM-poh ah-ee stoo-DYAH-toh leen-GLEH-seh?*
Have you studied English in America or in the U.K.?	**Hai studiato inglese in America o in Inghilterra?** *ah-ee stoo-DYAH-toh een-GLEH-seh een ah-MEH-ree-kah oh een een-geel-TEHR-rah?*
Say something.	**Dì qualcosa.** *dee kwahl-KOH-zah.*
What are you talking about?	**Di cosa stai parlando?** *dee KOH-zah stah-ee pahr-LAHN-doh?*

This sentence could be interpreted either as a real question to clarify something that is not clear, or as a veiled accusation used to criticize the speaker. Everything will depend on the tone of voice and non-verbal cues.

Let's keep talking about it.	**Continuiamo a discutere.** *kohn-tee-noo-YAH-moh ah dee-skoo-TEH-reh.*
Let's talk about it later.	**Parliamone dopo.** *pahr-lyah-MOH-neh DOH-poh.*

I don't want to talk.	**Non voglio parlare.** *nohn VOH-lyoh pahr-LAH-reh.*
I don't want to talk about it.	**Non voglio parlare di questo.** *nohn VOH-lyoh pahr-LAH-reh dee KWEH-stoh.*
By the way…	**A proposito…** *ah proh-POH-zee-toh…*
Just to change the subject…	**Per cambiare argomento…** *pehr kahm-BYAH-reh ahr-goh-MEHN-toh…*

In a situation that is becoming tense, especially with someone they are not intimate with, Italians would try to lighten up the mood with a joke, or by inviting you to relax, or by changing the subject. Some good sentences for these are:

Please, do not get upset…	**Sù non ti arrabbiare…** *soo nohn tee ahr-rah-BYAH-reh…*
Nice weather…	**Bella giornata…** *BEHL-lah jyoor-NAH-tah…*
When are you going on vacation?	**Quando vai in vacanza?** *KWAHN-doh vah-ee een vah-KAHN-tsah?*
It is getting late… / I need to go.	**È tardi… / devo andare.** *eh TAHR-dee… / DEH-voh ahn-DAH-reh.*

But of course there are situations in which the argument cannot be avoided, and the discussion gets heated. And in truth Italians love to passionately defend their point of view about...everything. Be mindful that in Italian culture to "argue" even publicly—to raise your voice and become very assertive—is not taken as an impolite or rude behavior, but simply a pretty routine one. Here we go:

Do not make excuses.	**Non cercare scuse.** *nohn chehr-KAH-reh SKOO-zeh.*
That's not a good excuse.	**Questa non è una buona scusa.** *KWEH-stah nohn eh oo-nah BWOH-nah SKOO-zah.*
Stop complaining!	**Smettila di lamentarti!** *SMEHT-tee-lah dee lah-mehn-TAHR-tee!*

You will hear the first part of this exclamation, **Smettila** (meaning "Stop it"), all the time in Italy. It's part of the normal back and forth in an argument or disagreement, in a couple's discussion, in television talk shows, or when parents try to make their children stay quiet and stop doing something annoying.

Do you know what you are saying?	**Hai un'idea di cosa stai dicendo?** *ah-ee oon ee-DAY-ah dee KOH-zah stah-ee dee-CHEHN-doh?*

A hostile phrase expressing disbelief and destined to trigger a reaction in the other person.

You said that, didn't you?

Lo hai detto tu, o no?
*Loh ah-ee DEHT-toh too,
oh noh?*

I didn't say anything.

Non ho detto niente.
*nohn oh DEHT-toh
NYEHN-teh.*

You'd better not say things
like that.

**Fai meglio a non dire
cose così / queste cose.**
*fah-ee MEH-lyoh ah nohn
DEE-reh KOH-zeh koh-ZEE /
KWEH-steh KOH-zeh.*

Don't say things like that.

**Non dire cose così /
queste cose.**
*nohn DEE-reh KOH-zeh koh-ZEE /
KWEH-steh KOH-zeh.*

Don't talk so loudly.

Non alzare la voce.
*nohn ahl-TSAH-reh lah
VOH-cheh.*

Again: This sentence is used all the time because everyone
yells in Italy, and as a natural consequence everyone starts
speaking very loudly to be heard. You'll often see groups of
people talking all at the same time, raising their voices over

each other, and they can look very agitated and emotional: but do not worry, it is just normal in Italy and it does not mean that a real argument is going on. They are simply making their points. If you somehow do not have this experience in person, just turn on the television while in Italy and follow a talk show; you will see each of the participants, be they simple citizens or congressmen, blue collar workers or dignitaries, at some point screaming together. The same scene can be seen even in the recording of a Parliament session: politics and passion go hand in hand in Italy!

Coming and Going
Andare e Venire 6

Come here.

Vieni qui.
VYEH-nee kwee.

Come over.

Vieni vicino a me.
VYEH-nee vee-CHEE-noh ah meh.

Come later.

Vieni più tardi.
VYEH-nee pyoo TAHR-dee.

Can you come?

Puoi venire?
pwoy veh-NEE-reh?

Won't you come with
me / us?

**Non vuoi venire con me /
noi?**
*nohn vwoy veh-NEE-reh kohn
meh / nwoy?*

She / he is coming here.

Lei / lui sta venendo qui.
*leh-ee / loo-ee stah
veh-NEHN-doh kwee.*

Lei / lui are the pronouns: feminine ("she") and masculine
("he").

I am coming, wait a second.

Vengo, aspetta un attimo.
*VEHN-goh, ah-SPEHT-tah oon
AHT-tee-moh.*

I can go.

Posso andare.
POHS-soh ahn-DAH-reh.

I think I can go.

Penso di poter andare.
*PEHN-soh dee POH-tehr
ahn-DAH-reh.*

I can't go.

Non posso andare.
nohn POHS-soh ahn-DAH-reh.

I want to go.

Voglio andare.
VOH-lyoh ahn-DAH-reh.

To say **voglio**, pronounce the **gl** like the **lli** in "million."

I want to go to Rome /
Venice / Florence.

**Voglio andare a Roma /
Venezia / Firenze.**
*VOH-lyoh ahn-DAH-reh ah
ROH-mah / veh-NEE-tsyah /
fee-REHN-tseh.*

I really want to go.

Voglio proprio andare.
*VOH-lyoh PROH-pree-oh
ahn-DAH-reh.*

I don't want to go.

Non voglio andare.
nohn VOH-lyoh ahn-DAH-reh.

You went, didn't you?

Sei andato, vero?
seh-ee ahn-DAH-toh, VEH-roh?

I went.

Sono andato.
SOH-noh ahn-DAH-toh.

I didn't go.

Non ci sono andato.
nohn chee SOH-noh
ahn-DAH-toh.

Don't go yet.

Aspetta ad andare.
ah-SPEHT-tah ahd ahn-DAH-reh.

Don't go.

Non andare.
nohn ahn-DAH-reh.

I must go now.

Devo andare adesso.
deh-voh ahn-DAH-reh
ah-DEHS-soh.

May I go?

Posso andare?
POHS-soh ahn-DAH-reh?

Shall we go?

Andiamo?
ahn-DYAH-moh?

Let's go.

Andiamo.
ahn-DYAH-moh.

Notice that the two sentences above are translated in Italian in the same identical way, with a single verb. The only way to tell them apart will be through the tone of voice and the posture of the speaker. But do not worry in the least: you will easily recognize the meaning of the sentence. Italians put a lot of non-verbal expression in their words; try to do the same in order to be understood.

Let's leave / let's get out of here.

Andiamo via da qui.
ahn-DYAH-moh VEE-ah
dah kwee.

I am leaving soon.

Me ne andrò fra poco.
meh neh ahn-DROH
frah POH-koh.

Fra poco is the equivalent of "in a little while," "soon." It is a handy little expression for travellers; you can use it to let the hotel people know you are on the verge of leaving the room, for example, or when you're calling for a taxi.

She / he has left here.

Lei / lui se ne è andata/o da qui.
leh-ee / loo-ee seh neh eh ahn-DAH-tah/toh dah kwee.

She / he has gone home.

Lei / lui è andata/o a casa.
leh-ee / loo-ee eh ahn-DAH-tah/toh ah KAH-zah.

Where are you going?

Dove stai andando?
DOH-veh stah-ee ahn-DAHN-doh?

Please go first / After you.

Prego, dopo di te / lei.
PREH-goh, DOH-poh dee teh / leh-ee.

You will use the **te** form of this sentence in every informal conversation, or the **lei** form in the more formal situations with someone you are not intimate with, and you will hear people using the **lei** with you when they want to be particularly respectful.

Thanks for letting me
go first.

Grazie per avermi fatto passare prima.
GRAH-tsyeh pehr ah-VEHR-mee FAHT-toh pahs-SAH-reh PREE-mah.

Take your time. /
Go slowly.

**Non avere fretta. /
Vai piano.**
nohn ah-VEH-reh FREHT-tah. /
vah-ee pee-AH-noh.

I'm lost.

Mi sono persa/o.
mee SOH-noh PEHR-sah/soh.

Please tell me the way.

**Per favore, mi può dire
dove devo andare?**
pehr fah-VOH-reh, mee pwoh
DEE-reh DOH-veh
DEH-voh ahn-DAH-reh?

Of course you can ask this question only after having explained where you are supposed to go or while you are showing a map.

Could you write it down?

**Può scrivere le indicazioni
per favore?**
pwoh skree-VEH-reh leh
een-dee-kah-TSYOH-nee
pehr fah-VOH-reh?

Please tell me the train
station name.

**Per favore dimmi / mi dica
il nome della stazione?**
pehr fah-VOH-reh
DEEM-mee / mee DEE-kah
eel NOH-meh DEHL-lah
stah-TSYOH-neh?

Dimmi is the informal **tu** way to say this. If you want to be more formal, instead use the **lei** form: **mi dica....**

Which train / bus should I take?	**Quale treno / autobus devo prendere?** *KWAH-leh TREH-noh / OH-toh-boos DEH-voh prehn-DEH-reh?*
Get off at [train station]… / [bus stop]…	**Scendi alla stazione di… / alla fermata di…** *SEHN-dee AHL-lah stah-TSYOH-neh dee… / AHL-lah fehr-MAH-tah dee…*

The word **stazione** used by itself always refers to the train station and it is usually indicated with the name of the town it is in, as in "Stazione di Bologna." Sometimes a Catholic saint's name is used, for example, Stazione di Firenze S. Maria Novella.

Stazione degli autobus is instead the bus station. Note that this type of "stazione" will always be specified "**degli autobus**."

Fermata is the word used for the bus stop and it is usually indicated with the name of a street, a square, or an ancient doorway (we are in Italy where cities are surrounded by walls and, of course, some doors).

How will I know when
to get off?

**Come faccio sapere dove
devo scendere?**
*KOH-meh FAH-chyoh sah-PEH-
reh DOH-veh DEH-voh
sehn-DEH-reh?*

You will hear the station
name announced on the
train. / If you are on a
bus you'd better ask the
bus driver.

**Sentirai il nome della
stazione in treno. /
Se sei su un autobus è
meglio chiedere al
conducente.**
*sehn-TEE-reh eel NOH-meh
DEHL-lah stah-TSYOH-neh
een TREH-noh. / seh seh-ee
soo oon OH-toh-boos eh
MEH-lyoh kyeh-DEH-reh
ahl kohn-doo-SEHN-teh.*

How much does the
ticket / ride cost?

**Quanto costa il biglietto /
la corsa?**
*KWAHN-toh KOH-stah eel
bee-LYEHT-toh /
lah KOHR-sah?*

I'll be waiting in front of
the station / at the
bus stop.

**Ti aspetto di fronte alla
stazione / alla fermata
dell'autobus.**
*tee ah-SPEHT-toh dee
FROHN-teh AHL-lah
stah-TSYOH-neh /
AHL-lah fehr-MAH-tah
dehl-LOH-toh-boos.*

Eat, Drink, Be Merry
Mangia, Bevi, Goditi la Vita

Goditi la vita (enjoy life) is not only a common expression and a wish in Italy, but it is a concept associated with having good food and good wine. Italian culture is the very definition of a food culture, with all possible attention devoted not only to food preparation but to the constant search for the best, most natural, and tastiest ingredients.

When people meet they immediately offer each other a coffee, a cappuccino or an **aperitivo** (drink before dinner which can be alcoholic or not), and often they invite each other over for a meal. Italians invite friends and family for lunch and dinner regularly, often on a weekly basis. Even at the end of a workday a relaxing evening entails a good homecooked dinner or a simple gathering in a good **trattoria** (usually a neighborhood-based, cheerful little restaurant). Every event of human life is marked with an eating feast in Italy: from the baptism of a newborn to First Communions, birthdays, weddings, funerals, dating, arrivals and departures of friends and relatives. Important discussions or relaxing conversations take place around a table and last for hours; Sunday's lunch can easily go from 1:00 to 5:30 p.m. Dinners can last from 8:30 to 11 p.m., especially in the south where the tendency toward late meals is more marked.

In Italy you'll be better prepared if you know a few of the differences—aside of course from the ones about food choices and combinations—from American meals. For one thing, breakfast in Italy (called **prima colazione** or simply

colazione) is a very light meal; you'll have only an espresso coffee, a cappuccino or a caffelatte, usually with a pastry, a croissant or just a couple of cookies. No proteins, meat, fruits, juices, etc.

Also, you will not find the equivalent of the American barbecue or cookout. Italians do not barbecue. Usually it's simply because they do not have backyards since they mainly live in apartment buildings.

Instead they cook and offer the most delicious, simple and tasteful food in the Italian way. Here are the two words you'll need to enjoy an Italian meal at home or at a restaurant: **pranzo** (lunch); **cena** (dinner).

I am hungry.	**Ho fame.** *oh FAH-meh.*
I'd like to eat something.	**Vorrei mangiare qualcosa.** *VOHR-reh mahn-JYAH-reh* *kwahl-KOH-zah.*
I haven't eaten yet.	**Non ho ancora mangiato.** *nohn oh ahn-KOH-rah* *mahn-JYAH-toh.*
Do you want to eat?	**Vuoi mangiare qualcosa?** *vwoy mahn-JYAH-reh* *kwahl-KOH-zah?*
I don't want to eat now.	**Non voglio mangiare adesso.** *nohn VOH-lyoh mahn-JYAH-reh* *ah-DEHS-soh.*
Did you eat lunch / dinner?	**Hai pranzato / Hai cenato?** *ah-ee prahn-TSAH-toh /* *ah-ee cheh-NAH-toh?*

In Italian you use a single word, a verb, to say either "have lunch" or "have dinner," respectively: **pranzare** or **cenare**.

What would you like?

Cosa desideri?
KOH-zah deh-zee-DEH-ree?

I am thirsty.

Ho sete.
oh SEH-teh.

Ho (I have) **sete** (thirst). In Italian you express feelings of hunger and thirst with the verb "to have": again, Italians profoundly "own" their feelings.

I'd like some wine / a beer.

Vorrei un po' di vino / una birra.
VOHR-reh oon poh dee VEE-noh / oo-nah BEE-rah.

I'd like a soft drink / cola / coffee / tea / green tea.

Vorrei un analcolico / una Coca-Cola / un caffè / un tè / un tè verde.
VOHR-reh oon ahn-ahl-KOH-lee-koh / oo-nah Coca-Cola / oon kahf-FEH / oon teh / oon teh VEHR-deh.

All the above drinks are commonly found in Italy, but of course the universally beloved one is coffee. Italians are espresso lovers and espresso-dependent; the short, tasty, thick coffee typical of the Italian tradition is an important part of daily life. Italians start with espresso in the morning.

Often they have one or two more during the morning; and **"il caffettino dopo pranzo"** (after lunch) is mandatory. For the bravest who don't suffer from insomnia the espresso drinking goes on in the midafternoon until after dinner.

Tea drinking is also common, both in the morning and in the afternoon. However it is still very rare to see people walking around the Italian streets or squares carrying a bottle of water, as is done in the U.S. If you do that while visiting Italy, you may secretly be glanced at as being a bit strange, perhaps suffering from some phobia of being lost in a desert. In Italy this risk does not exist: there is a **bar** (coffee shop) every few meters, with all the water you could possibly need.

I don't want to drink.	**Non ho voglia di bere.** *nohn oh VOH-lyah dee BEH-reh.*
I haven't had anything to drink yet.	**Non ho ancora preso niente da bere.** *nohn oh ahn-KOH-rah PREH-zoh NYEHN-teh dah BEH-reh.*
Do you want to drink something?	**Vuoi bere qualcosa?** *vwoy BEH-reh kwahl-KOH-zah?*
Do you want to drink some more?	**Ancora qualcosa da bere?** *ahn-KOH-rah kwahl-KOH-zah dah BEH-reh?*
Thank you but I still have some.	**Grazie, ma ho ancora da bere.** *GRAH-tsyeh, mah oh ahn-KOH-rah dah BEH-reh.*

Here are the sentences you will need to know when having lunch or dinner in Italy, in a restaurant or in a home.

How about some lunch / dinner?

Andiamo a pranzo/a cena?
ahn-DYAH-moh ah PRAHN-tsoh/tsah CHEH-nah?

Shall we go to a restaurant, a pizzeria, or a trattoria?

Andiamo in un ristorante, in una pizzeria, o in una trattoria?
ahn-DYAH-moh een oon ree-stoh-RAHN-teh, een oo-nah pee-tseh-REE-ah, oh een oo-nah traht-toh-REE-ah?

Everyone asks this question for a first general narrowing-down about what kind of meal and ambiance to choose, since there are clear differences among these three kinds of places.

A **ristorante** is usually a more elegant place with white tablecloths, attentive waiters, higher prices; a simple **trattoria** is a neighborhood restaurant, more casual, family owned with wood tables and sometimes only paper tablecloths but still delicious food for a cheaper price; a pizzeria is of course where pizza is the specialty. Often signs will say "**Trattoria-Pizzeria**," indicating a place where the food choices of both are combined.

Very rarely will you find a rigid dress code in Italy. Consider that Italians almost always favor a more casual-chic style of clothing and judge it a bit unsophisticated to dress in a too-precise way. But of course if you go to a nice restaurant you would feel most comfortable wearing a nice dress (women) or a blazer or suit with or without tie (men).

Have you ordered?

Hai ordinato?
ah-ee ohr-dee-NAH-toh?

Do you prefer meat or fish?　**Preferesci carne o pesce?**
preh-feh-REH-shee KAHR-neh
oh PEH-sheh?

This very question is usually asked before deciding upon the restaurant. And in any case as soon as people sit down in the chosen restaurant the waiter will ask it again, in order to help with the choice of the right wine and the best food combinations.

Do you want a first course?　**Vuoi un primo piatto?**
vwoy oon PREE-moh PYAHT-toh?

This question will always be asked in an Italian restaurant or trattoria. In Italy a meal is composed of an appetizer (antipasto), first course (pasta), second course or **secondo** (fish, meat, cheese), side vegetable or **contorno**, and dessert, **dolce**: a full meal is a five-course one. Also, on the price front, keep in mind that unlike the norm in the U.S., in Italy the **contorno** (side vegetable) is never included in the main course and you will have to pay separately for it.

However nowadays many people try to eat *only* a pasta or a **secondo**, not both. That's why the waiter will want to know if you want to start your meal with a pasta and then pass to the meat or fish course, or if you want to skip pasta and start directly with the **secondo**.

The following are questions that can be used either in a public place (ristorante, pizzeria, trattoria) or when you are invited into an Italian home for a meal.

Will you try this (food)?　**Vuoi provare questo?**
vwoy proh-VAH-reh KWEH-stoh?

Try this?　**Prova questo?**
PROH-vah KWEH-stoh?

What's it called?

Come si chiama?
KOH-meh see KYAH-mah?

I've never tried…

Non ho mai provato…
nohn oh mah-ee proh-VAH-toh…

What's your favorite
Italian food?

**Qual'è il tuo piatto
italiano preferito?**
*KWAHL ay eel too-oh
PYAHT-toh ee-tah-LYAH-noh
preh-feh-REE-toh?*

In Italian to talk about your favorites or not-favorites you
use the word "dish" (**piatto**) instead of "food."

Can you eat meat or fish,
or you are vegetarian?

**Mangi carne o pesce o
sei vegetariano/a?**
*MAHN-jee KAHR-neh oh
PEH-skeh oh seh-ee
veh-jeh-tah-RYAH-noh/nah?*

Because most Italian dishes, including pasta ones, come with
meat or fish sauces, it is common to make sure before serv-
ing it that someone is not vegetarian.

Yes, I can eat meat / fish.

Sì, mangio carne / pesce.
*see, MAHN-jyoh
KAHR-neh/PEH-skeh.*

No, I am vegetarian.

No, sono vegetariano/a.
noh, SOH-noh
veh-jeh-tah-RYAH-noh/nah.

(That) looks delicious.

Sembra delizioso.
SEHM-brah
deh-lee-TSYOH-zoh.

It smells good.

Ha un buon odore.
hah oon bwohn oh-DOH-reh.

Give me more.

Dammene un po' di più.
DAHM-meh-neh oon poh
dee pyoo.

Enough.

È abbastanza.
eh ahb-bah-STAHN-tsah.

Enough?

Abbastanza?
ahb-bah-STAHN-tsah?

Not enough.

Non abbastanza.
nohn ahb-bah-STAHN-tsah.

Do you want some more?

Ne vuoi un po' di più?
neh vwoy oon poh dee pyoo?

In an Italian home you will be asked over and over again if you want some more of whatever is being served. They will ask you if you want more **pasta, carne, pesce**, dessert, and after the dessert you will be offered fruits, and after that cheese, and then coffee, and to finish some liquor. You can only say with a smile **"Basta, grazie"** (Enough, thanks!).

Sorry, I can't eat that.

Mi dispiace, ma non posso mangiare quel ___ .
mee dees-PYAH-cheh, mah nohn POHS-soh mahn-JYAH-reh kwehl ___ .

You will need to add the precise name of the food after **quel** that you can't eat, otherwise the sentence will remain unclear.

Buon appetito!   *bwohn ahp-peh-TEE-toh!*

Learn this sentence and use it! When you say it you will be looked upon as admirably trying to plug into the Italian food culture. "**Buon appetito**" is used at the beginning of every meal and it is a wish for everyone at the table to maintain and enjoy a good appetite.

Do you like it?

Ti piace?
tee PYAH-cheh?

It tastes good.

Ha un buon sapore.
hah oon bwohn sah-POH-reh.

You can reply to the **Ti piace?** question, that indeed "**Ha un buon sapore.**"

It's an unusual taste.

È un sapore strano / curioso.
eh oon sah-POH-reh STRAH-noh / koo-RYOH-soh.

It's okay / so-so.

Va bene / È così così.
vah BEH-neh / eh koh-ZEE koh-ZEE.

It's not good.

Non è buono.
nohn eh BWOH-noh.

It does not taste good.	**Non ha un buon sapore.** *nohn ah oon bwohn* *sah-POH-reh.*
It's awful.	**È cattivo.** *eh kaht-TEE-voh.*
I'm full.	**Sono piena/o.** *SOH-noh PYEH-nah/noh.*

Indeed this happens quite often in Italy. The good side of this "being full" feeling is that usually the food eaten is very genuine, with few additives, and neither hormones nor vitamins added. On top of that, gaining weight while in Italy is actually not so easy since everyone walks a lot.

Likes and Dislikes
Mi Piace, Non Mi Piace   8

I like it.	**Mi piace.** *mee PYAH-cheh.*
I like it a lot.	**Mi piace molto.** *mee PYAH-cheh MOHL-toh.*
I love it.	**Lo / la adoro.** *loh / lah ah-DOH-roh.*

In Italian, the closest equivalent of the "I love" or the "love ya" so generally used in America could be "I adore," which is a stronger word. But it also has a playful connotation, almost that of a very sweet, smiling exaggeration. You can "adore" a landscape, a friend, a food, a painting, a book, a movie, a job, a trip. Remember: Italians can be playful and dramatic and passionate, but they save several specific expressions for their romantic partners.

Italians use the literal expression "I love" (**lo/la amo**) almost only when referring to a romantic partner, a fiance, a wife, a husband: romantic love occupies a unique, untouchable place in Italian culture and with it comes a whole set of words related exclusively to it.

They do not use the verb "love" toward their children, their friends or their family. There are not Hallmark cards in Italy for Valentine's Day with the word "love" for friends, girlfriends, or neighbors. Italians do not end a letter or a note or a phone call with the word "love". Love in Italy is all about romantic love. Naturally when you court someone or you are courted you will hear, or use, that term. But for other loved ones, as for family members, Italians use "**ti voglio bene**" (I care for you, or literally "I want your good.").

On the other hand, the way to end a note, a letter, or an e-mail in Italy is, most of the time, "**Baci e Abbracci**" (hugs and kisses): so...Italians hug and kiss everybody but they are very careful whom they "love."

It's okay / so-so.	**Va bene / È così-così** *vah BEH-neh /* *eh koh-ZEE koh-ZEE.*
I don't like it very much.	**Non mi piace molto.** *nohn mee PYAH-cheh* *MOHL-toh.*
I don't like it at all.	**Non mi piace per niente.** *nohn mee PYAH-cheh pehr* *NYEHN-teh.*
I hate it.	**Lo odio. / lo detesto.** *loh OH-dyoh. /* *loh deh-TEH-stoh.*
I really hate it.	**Lo odio proprio /** **Mi fa schifo.** *loh OH-dyoh PROH-pree-oh. /* *mee fah SHEE-foh.*

Lo odio proprio mirrors the English "I really hate it" and you can use it accordingly. But it is quite common in Italian to use the stronger and in a way more rude expression **Mi fa schifo** which expresses almost a physical revulsion toward something, someone, an activity, a place, a smell. It is very common to hear this phrase; it has a caricature-like tone and can be used as the opposite of "I adore it."

I want...	**Voglio...** *VOH-lyoh...*
I really want...	**Voglio proprio...** *VOH-lyoh PROH-pree-oh...*
I don't want...	**Non voglio...** *nohn VOH-lyoh...*
I really don't want...	**Non voglio proprio...** *nohn VOH-lyoh PROH-pree-oh...*
I'm busy.	**Sono occupato/a.** *SOH-noh ohk-koo-PAH-toh/tah.*
I'm happy.	**Sono felice.** *SOH-noh feh-LEE-cheh.*
I'm glad to know that...	**Sono lieto di sapere che...** *SOH-noh LYEH-toh dee sah-PEH-reh kay...*
I am sad.	**Sono triste.** *SOH-noh TREE-steh.*
I'm fine.	**Sto bene.** *stoh BEH-neh.*

I'm mad. / I'm mad at you.	**Sono arrabbiato/a. / Sono arrabbiato/a con te.** *SOH-noh ahr-rahb-BYAH-toh/tah. / SOH-noh ahr-rahb-BYAH-toh/tah kohn teh.*
I'm ready.	**Sono pronto/a.** *SOH-noh PROHN-toh/tah.*
I'm tired.	**Sono stanco/a.** *SOH-noh STAHN-koh/kah.*
I'm surprised / What a surprise.	**Non me lo aspettavo / Che sorpresa!** *nohn meh loh ah-speht-TAH-voh / keh sohr-PREH-zah!*
What a relief.	**Che sollievo.** *keh soh-LYEH-voh.*
I'm scared.	**Sono spaventato/a.** *SOH-noh spah-vehn-TAH-toh/tah.*
I feel sick.	**Mi sento male.** *mee SYEHN-toh MAH-leh.*
I'm disappointed.	**Sono seccato/a.** *SOH-noh sehk-KAH-toh/tah.*

To express disappointment the Italian language uses the verb **seccare**, which literally means "to dry up," to express physically the feeling of disappointment that doesn't leave any warm, soft, moist emotions left inside.

I was worried.	**Ero preoccupato/a.** *EH-roh preh-ohk-koo-PAH-toh/ tah.*
Can't you do it?	**Non puoi farlo?** *non pwoy FAHR-loh?*
I can do it.	**Posso farlo.** *POHS-soh FAHR-loh.*
I can't do it.	**Non posso farlo.** *nohn POHS-soh FAHR-loh.*
Sorry. I can't.	**Mi dispiace. Non posso.** *mee dee-SPYAH-cheh. non POHS-soh.*
I'll do it.	**Lo farò.** *loh fah-ROH.*
I'm tired of...	**Sono stanco di...** *SOH-noh STAHN-koh dee...*

(At the end of this phrase, state whatever it is you're tired of.)

I understand.	**Capisco.** *kah-PEE-skoh.*
I understand very well.	**Capisco benissimo.** *kah-PEE-skoh beh-NEES-see-moh.*
I think I understand.	**Credo di capire.** *KREH-doh dee kah-PEE-reh.*

I don't understand.

Non capisco.
nohn kah-PEE-skoh.

I don't understand very well.

Non capisco bene.
nohn kah-PEE-skoh BEH-neh.

I know that person.

Conosco quella persona.
*koh-NOH-skoh KWEHL-lah
pehr-SOH-nah.*

The Italian language has two different verbs to translate the
English "to know." There is **sapere** which equals to "to be
knowledgeable about something" as when you have studied
something; and there is **conoscere** which has the meaning
"to know someone." Notice the difference, in the following
phrases.

Do you know that person?

Lo / La conosci?
loh / lah koh-NOH-shee?

Ah, you know that person.

Ah, lo / la conosci.
ah, loh / lah koh-NOH-shee.

I know.

Lo so.
loh soh.

I don't know.

Non so.
nohn soh.

You knew that, didn't you? **Lo sapevi, non è vero?**
loh sah-PEH-vee,
nohn eh VEH-roh?

Give me time to think **Dammi tempo di pensarci**
it over. **sù.**
DAHM-mee TEHM-poh dee
pehn-SAHR-chee soo.

I'll think about it. **Ci penserò.**
chee pehn-seh-ROH.

I'm so confused. **Sono così confuso/a.**
SOH-noh koh-ZEE
kohn-FOO-zoh/zah.

I made a mistake. **Ho sbagliato. /**
Ho fatto uno sbaglio.
oh sbah-LYAH-toh. / oh FAHT-
toh oo-noh SBAH-lyoh.

These two sentences are equivalent; use either.

I blew it. **Ho sbagliato tutto.**
oh sbah-LYAH-toh TOOT-toh.

Am I right? **Ho ragione?**
oh rah-JYOH-neh?

Am I wrong? **Sbaglio? / Ho torto?**
SBAH-lyoh? / oh TOHR-toh?

What a pity / too bad. **Che peccato.**
keh pehk-KAH-toh.

I hope so.

Spero di sì.
SPEH-roh dee SEE.

Go. Go for it (Good luck)

Provaci. (Buona fortuna)
*proh-VAH-chee. (BWOH-nah
fohr-TOO-nah)*

Calm down.

Calmati.
KAHL-mah-tee.

Cheer up.

Tirati sù.
TEE-rah-tee soo.

Never mind.

Non importa.
nohn eem-POHR-tah.

Cool.

Alla moda.
AHL-lah MOH-dah.

What a true-to-culture expression. Italians are more than just fashion-conscious; they consider themselves fashion-creators, the world's fashion **avanguarde**, the trend-setters. So it's only logical that to say "cool," Italians use a fashion-industry expression that means "trendy right now." **Alla moda** means it is trendy in this precise present season—and as you may know, the fashion season lasts only a few short months.

To be "cool" in the way you dress can be expensive in Italy. Italians follow the everchanging trends in clothing very closely, including the color combinations but also the new fashions in sunglasses, purses, shoes, watches, jewelry, hair-cuts, haircolor, belts, and so on and on…all "cool" one season and "uncool" the following one.

Uncool.	**Fuori moda.**
	FWOH-ree MOH-dah.

Here it is, just as you expected: "uncool" is expressed with "*out* of the present fashion trend."

Awesome.	**Meraviglioso / Incredibile.**
	meh-rah-vee-LYOH-soh /
	een-kreh-dee-BEE-leh.

Cute.	**Carino/a.**
	kah-REE-noh/nah.

Really cute.	**Carinissimo/a.**
	kah-ree-NEES-see-moh/mah.

Clever. / Smart.	**Intelligente. / Sveglio.**
	een-tehl-lee-JEHN-teh /
	SVEH-lyoh.

While the word **intelligente** works exactly as the English equivalent, **sveglio** is a more colloquial word meaning "a bit *too* smart"; you might use it when you want to be a little sarcastic.

Ugly.	**Orribile.**
	ohr-ree-BEE-leh.

Smart ass.	**Furbo/a. / Paraculo/a.**
	FOOR-boh/bah. / pah-rah-KOO-
	loh/lah.

Furbo ("smart") is the correct, clean Italian version of this sentiment, implying clever and perhaps a bit slick.

Paraculo, on the other hand, is not an elegant word, and it would be advisable not to use it in formal conversation. But this slang expression has stepped into more general use in recent years, and it is a very common one that visitors will hear all the time, referring to persons who are very smart and a little malicious. It is more ironic than offensive.

Insults and Quarrels
Insulti e Litigi

9

It is important that you understand a notable difference between Italian and American culture: in Italy you may see or hear a group of people, or even just two people, speaking very loudly or clearly screaming at each other on the street, at a corner, in line, in a **caffè**, in a restaurant (wherever), and assume they are in the middle of a nasty fight. Not true: most of the time, meaning 90 or 95% of the time, what you are witnessing is *not* at all a dramatic fight. It is just a quarrel, a passing disagreement, the statement of different points of view; Italians are simply very expressive and direct in their communication style. They can turn red in the face, move their hands in strange gestures and yell a lot, but after ten minutes they have forgotten all about it. Very very rarely will you see an actual, dangerous fight in an Italian public place. Of course, that does not mean that you should not pay attention. Always be mindful when walking at night in solitary alleys, or even in full daylight: in Italy the danger is often **scippi** or street thieves, unarmed, running next to you and grabbing your purse or wallet or necklace, in front of everyone.

But most of the time Italian streets are a theater of very innocuous arguments.

These are the phrases that you may hear in different situations during your travels including the classic one in which someone tries to "steal" the spot in the front of a line. Be prepared: Italians do *not* respect lines. When you walk into a crowded coffee shop, pharmacy, or store, you will see an unruly group of people around the front desk trying to be served and quarreling with each other.

We're making a line.

Siamo in coda qui.
SYAH-moh een KOH-dah kwee.

Don't push.

Non spingere.
nohn speen-JEH-reh.

This sentence will be a daily occurrence in your Italian trip. Italian streets are narrow and crowded, and feeling pushed happens often, no matter whether in a supermarket or at a train station or even outdoors, taking a stroll in the populated cobblestone street of a town center.

Man, they are slow.

Sono così lenti.
SOH-noh koh-ZEE LEHN-tee.

Could you go a little faster.

Può andare più veloce.
pwoh ahn-DAH-reh pyoo veh-LOH-cheh.

The service here is so bad.

Il servizio qui è pessimo.
eel sehr-VEE-tsyoh kwee eh PEHS-see-moh.

Do you want to say something?

Vuoi dire qualcosa?
vwoy DEE-reh kwahl-KOH-zah?

Don't look at me.

Non mi guardare.
nohn mee gwahr-DAH-reh.

Italians usually look directly at other people and do not find it disturbing to be looked at. So this is a rare phrase to hear in Italy, but it can happen at times.

Don't stare at me.   **Non mi fissare.**
                                  nohn mee fees-SAH-reh.

When in Italy just try to get used to being stared at. If you
are a woman and a man stares at you do not take it as a
vulgar act, because in Italy it is normal. Men look at women
simply to express their admiration, to start a conversation,
and only at times to begin a real courtship. It can also happen that they pay you a verbal compliment like **"Bellezza"**
("beauty!"); accept it with a smile and move on if you are
not interested.

Women also stare at men but not so often, because
Italian women are fairly traditional when it comes to
romantic relationships and they enjoy being courted. The
more common thing is to see women staring at other
women: they are just studying their fashion style or makeup.

Pervert!   **Maniaco!**
                                  mah-NEE-ah-koh!

Vulgar!   **Volgare!**
                                  vohl-GAH-reh!

Take your hands off.   **Giù le mani!**
                                  JYOO leh MAH-nee!

If someone is touching you in an inappropriate way that you
believe is not by accident, maybe in a crowded bus, this is
the sentence to use. Be aware that this is a strong "command" phrase. You can use it also in more friendly contexts
(if children are touching the food before dinner, for
instance, you might say **"giù le mani da..."**). As always. the
non-verbal cues are going to be the key to understanding
what's going on.

Don't touch me.   **Non mi toccare.**
                                  nohn mee tohk-KAH-reh.

This can't be right.

Non è giusto.
nohn eh JYOO-stoh.

I think you are tricking me.

Mi stai prendendo in giro.
*mee stah-ee prehn-DEHN-doh
een JEE-roh.*

This is an idiomatic phrase that means literally "you are taking me around in circles" and that is used for multiple occasions, most of the time not for conflicts but for playfulness.
It can for example be used just to play modest, if someone
pays you a special compliment.

This can't be so expensive.

**Non può essere così
costoso / caro.**
*nohn pwoh ehs-SEH-reh
koh-ZEE koh-STOH-zoh /
KAH-roh.*

Costoso and **caro** both mean "expensive." Learn both these
words and use them freely if you think you have been over-
charged in a store, or in a restaurant, or even when you are
taking a cab, since taxi prices are often a problem in Italy
even though recently some progress has been made in fix-
ing a standard rate from some airports to town. But always
be upfront about the taxi fare: when jumping in a cab and
giving the driver the address you need to be taken to, ask
in advance how much the ride is going to be ("**Quanto mi
costera?**").

This is more expensive than
what I thought.

**È più caro di quello che
pensavo.**
*eh pyoo KAH-roh dee KWEHL-
loh kay pehn-SAH-voh.*

This is different from what I've heard.

Questo è diverso da quello che avevo capito.
KWEH-stoh eh dee-VEHR-soh dah KWEHL-loh kay ah-VEH-voh KAH-pee-toh.

Don't think I am stupid.

Non credere che (io) sia stupido/a.
nohn kreh-DEH-reh kay (yoh) syah STOO-pee-doh/dah.

In Italian the subject (in this case **io**, "I") is implied: it does not need to be expressed. So you can say this sentence with the **io** or without it.

Explain to me why.

Spiegami perchè.
SPEE-gah-mee pehr-KAY.

Don't you think you made a mistake?

Non credi di aver sbagliato?
nohn KREH-dee dee ah-VEHR sbah-LYAH-toh?

Is this because I am a foreigner?

È perchè sono straniero/a?
eh pehr-KAY SOH-noh strah-NYEH-roh/rah?

Is this because I am an American?

È perchè sono americano/a?
eh pehr-KAY SOH-noh ah-meh-ree-KAH-noh/nah?

Learn this sentence just in case, but try not to use it unless someone has overtly accused you of something precisely because you are an American. Italians generally like Americans: older Italians have fond memories of the American liberation after World War II and still feel grateful toward the U.S., and many Italian youth like the American movie and music pop culture. Of course, some people have mixed feelings, exactly like some Americans have mixed feelings toward Europeans, especially for political reasons (avoid like the plague political discussion in Italy…all Italians are very passionate about it), but overall you will be surprised by how many displays of affection you will get when you say you are American.

I want to talk to the manager.	**Voglio parlare con il padrone / direttore.** *VOH-lyoh pahr-LAH-reh kohn eel pah-DROH-neh / dee-reht-TOH-reh.*

Padrone is the owner, and in Italy you usually ask to talk with the owner of a restaurant, pizzeria, store, etc., because in Italy the majority of the stores are individually owned. Only in a big hotel or in a public service office like a post office would you ask to talk to the "manager" (**direttore**).

I won't come here again.	**Non tornerò più qui.** *nohn tohr-neh-ROH pyoo kwee.*
I'll tell my friends.	**Lo dirò ai miei amici.** *loh dee-ROH ah-ee MYEH-ee ah-MEE-chee.*
Hey, tell me your name.	**Hei, come ti chiami?** *ay, KOH-meh tee KYAH-mee?*
You tried to trick me.	**Hai cercato di imbrogliarmi.** *ah-ee chehr-KAH-toh dee eem-broh-LYAHR-mee.*

You won't get away with this.   **Non te la caverai.**
                                nohn teh lah kah-veh-RAH-ee.

INSULTS & CURSES

These are the phrases that can be overheard during a more intense fight or argument in a public place. Rare, but still possible.

Damn it!   **Dannazione! / Mannaggia!**
                                dahn-nah-TSYOH-neh! /
                                mahn-NAH-djah!

Shit.   **Accidenti / Cazzo.**
                                ah-chee-DEHN-tee / KAH-tsoh.

Accidenti is the more educated word to use as a curse, while **cazzo** (lit. "penis") is clearly more vulgar but still widely used.

What a mess!   **Che casino!**
                                kay kah-SEE-noh!

Casino means literally "brothel" but this word has become common language even in most families' talk. You will hear it a lot, but be mindful not use it in formal occasions.

What do you want?   **Cosa vuoi?**
                                KOH-zah vwoy?

What did you say?   **Cosa hai detto?**
                                KOH-zah ah-ee DEHT-toh?

Who do you think you are?   **Chi credi di essere.**
                             kee KREH-dee dee
                             ehs-SEH-reh.

Commonly used among adults, when they are truly upset,
as well as when they are just joking. Again, pay attention to
the tone of voice and the facial expression to understand
what's really going on. Children also use this sentence while
playing or arguing with their peers.

Why do you talk like that   **Perchè mi parli così?**
   to me?   *pehr-KAY mee PAHR-lee*
                             koh-SEE?

Are you stupid or what?   **Sei stupido/a / cretino/a /**
                             deficiente / scemo/a?
                             seh-ee STOO-pee-doh/dah /
                             kreh-TEE-noh/nah /
                             day-fee-SYEHN-teh /
                             SHEH-moh/mah?

In Italian all these terms have the same meaning and are
used interchangeably: **stupido, cretino, deficiente, scemo.**

You're stupid.   **Tu sei stupido/a.**
                             too seh-ee STOO-pee-doh/dah.

You look stupid.

Sembri stupido/a.
SEHM-bree STOO-pee-doh/dah.

That's stupid.

Questo è stupido/a.
KWEH-stoh eh
STOO-pee-doh/dah.

What you did was stupid.

Hai fatto una cosa stupida.
ah-ee FAHT-toh oo-nah
KOH-zah STOO-pee-dah.

You are crazy.

Sei pazzo/a. / Sei matto/a.
seh-ee PAH-tsoh/tsah. /
seh-ee MAHT-toh/tah.

Pazzo and **matto** have an identical meaning.

Stop acting stupid /
Don't joke around
with me.

Smetti di fare lo stupido /
Non scherzare con me.
SMEHT-tee dee FAH-reh loh
STOO-pee-doh / nohn
skehr-TSAH-reh kohn meh.

Don't say stupid things.

Non dire cose stupide.
nohn DEE-reh KOH-zeh
STOO-pee-deh.

Liar.

Bugiardo/a.
boo-JAHR-doh/dah.

That's a lie.

È una bugia.
eh oo-nah BOO-jyah.

Don't lie.

Non dire bugie.
nohn DEE-reh BOO-jyeh.

Stop it.

Smettila!
SMEHT-tee-lah!

You shouldn't do that.

Non devi farlo.
nohn DEH-vee FAHR-loh.

Why do you do things
like that?

Perchè fai cose così?
*pehr-KAY fah-ee KOH-zeh
koh-ZEE?*

Leave him / her alone.

Lascialo / lasciala in pace.
*lah-SHYAH-loh/lah-SHYAH-lah
een PAH-cheh.*

Do as I say.

Fai quello che ti dico.
*fah-ee KWEHL-loh kay tee
DEE-koh.*

This is the limit.

Basta così.
BAH-stah koh-ZEE.

Not one word more.

Non una parola di più.
*nohn oo-nah pah-ROH-lah
dee pyoo.*

Give it back.

Ridammelo/la.
ree-DAHM-meh-loh/lah.

Leave me alone.

Lasciami solo/a.
lah-SHYAH-mee SOH-loh/lah.

Leave us alone.

Lasciaci soli/e.
lah-SHYAH-chee SOH-lee/leh.

Get out of here.

Vattene.
VAHT-teh-neh.

Come here.

Vieni qui.
VYEH-nee kwee.

You are loud.

Fai rumore.
fah-ee roo-MOH-reh.

Be quiet.

Stai tranquillo/a.
stah-ee trahn-KWEEL-loh/lah.

Shut up.

Taci.
TAH-chee.

It simply means "be silent" and it is not as rude as the
English "shut up". **Taci** can be used as an order, as a sign of
hostility or as a simple fact.

A very famous Italian poem, extremely musical and
romantic—"**La pioggia nel pineto**"—starts with the word
Taci.

You asshole.

Stronzo/a.
STROHN-tsoh/tsah.

Stronzo literally means "shit" and is used in Italy as "asshole" is used in the U.S.

You are ugly.

Sei brutto/a.
seh-ee BROOT-toh/tah.

You pig.

Maiale.
mah-YAH-leh.

Fag.

Frocio.
FROH-chyoh.

Don't fuck with me.　　　　　**Non mi provocare.**
　　　　　　　　　　　　　　nohn mee proh-voh-KAH-reh.

This Italian sentence is much more polite and usable in every occasion; it's not vulgar and hostile as the English phrase is.

Go to hell.　　　　　　　　　**Va all'inferno.**
　　　　　　　　　　　　　　vah ahl een-FEHR-noh.

Don't try to be cool.　　　　　**Non darti delle arie.**
　　　　　　　　　　　　　　nohn DAHR-tee DEHL-leh
　　　　　　　　　　　　　　ah-ryeh.

This is a very popular idiomatic phrase literally meaning "Do not put on too many airs around you."

Let's finish this now.　　　　　**Finiamola qui.**
　　　　　　　　　　　　　　fee-nyah-MOH-lah kwee.

In Italy, when calling a landline in a private home, or in an office, it's important to use these basic, polite phrases.

Hello.	**Pronto.** *PROHN-toh.*

Pronto (lit. "Ready"): this is the first word you'll hear when Italians answer the phone: they always use it when they receive a call and very often also when they place a call. Learn, and repeat: **Pronto.**

Good morning / good evening. Is _____ there please?	**Buongiorno / Buonasera.** **C'e _____ per favore?** *bwohn-JYOOR-noh / bwoh-nah-SEH-rah. chay _____* *pehr fah-VOH-reh?*
Could you get _____ please?	**Può chiamare _____ per favore?** *pwoh kyah-MAH-reh _____* *pehr fah-VOH-reh?*
Can I speak with _____?	**Posso parlare con _____?** *POHS-soh pahr-LAH-reh kohn _____?*

Hold on please.

Aspetti / attenda un attimo.
*ah-SPEHT-tee / aht-TEHN-dah
oon AHT-tee-moh.*

Hello, this is Robert;
can I please talk to
Maria?

**Pronto, sono Roberto;
posso per favore parlare
con Maria?**
*PROHN-toh, SOH-noh Roberto;
POHS-soh pehr fah-VOH-
reh pahr-LAH-reh kohn
Maria?*

Here she / he is.

Subito. Eccola/lo.
SOO-bee-toh. EHK-koh-lah/loh.

I am sorry, she / he is out.

Mi dispiace, lei / lui è fuori.
*mee dees-PYAH-cheh, leh-ee /
loo-ee eh FWOH-ree.*

She / he will be back later.

**Lei / Lui tornerà a casa più
tardi.**
*leh-ee / loo-ee tohr-neh-RAH
ah KAH-zah pyoo TAHR-
dee.*

Can I leave a message?

Posso lasciare un messaggio?
*POHS-soh lah-SHYAH-reh oon
mehs-SAH-djoh?*

Can you tell her / him
that Robert called?

**Può dirle / dirgli che Robert
ha chiamato?**
*pwoh DEER-leh / DEER-lyee
kay Robert ah
kyah-MAH-toh?*

This is the phone number where she / he can call me back...	**Questo è il telefono dove lei / lui mi può richiamare...** *KWEH-stoh eh eel teh-LEH-foh-noh DOH-veh leh-ee / loo-ee mee pwoh ree-kyah-MAH-reh...*
I'll tell her / him to call you back.	**Gli / le dirò di richiamarti.** *glyee / leh dee-ROH dee ree-kyah-MAHR-tee.*

CELL PHONES
Telefonini

Discussing **telefonini**—the Italian word for cell phones—means delving into an obsession shared by the entire population: Italians have embraced the use of cell phones beyond what most other nations can imagine. Back when they were still seen mainly as a worker's tool in the U.S., the Italians were already glued to them. And today most people have at least two cell phones (if not three): one for work, one for the family, and at times a third secret one....

There is no courtesy code in Italy concerning cell phone use. Everyone, everywhere speaks all the time on their **telefonino**, often loudly and about the most intimate events of their life, with absolute indifference to bystanders. On buses, in a taxi, in a train compartment, in line at the bank: there is noplace off limits for cell-phone talk in Italy.

Better be prepared; the concept of privacy is so limited in Italy, that in fact there is not a native word to express this concept, only an English one (**la privacy**). If you are out for dinner, for a coffee, for a date with someone, do not expect that they will turn off their phone. They will respond to a call no matter what.

And nowadays Italians have also thrown themselves into the world of text-messaging—when they are not speaking on their **telefonino**, they are sending messages, reading messages, responding to messages (sent to them most of the time by someone down the hall). Keep in mind that Italians communicate with each other on average on an hourly basis. They update each other on the smallest news and if there is no news, they just like to "touch base."

What kind of cell phone did you buy?	**Che cellulare hai comprato?** *kay chehl-loo-LAH-reh ah-ee kohm-PRAH-toh?*

This is really cute.	**È proprio carino.** *eh PROH-pree-oh kah-REE-noh.*

Carino is a nice word to learn and to use: it can be used as an adjective for an object but mainly for a person, and it is always a nice compliment to pay to someone. If you apply it to a person—as opposed to complimenting someone's cell phone—remember to say **carino** to a male, and **carina** to a female.

What's your e-mail address?	**Qual'è il tuo indirizzo di posta-elettronica?** *KWAH-leh eel too-oh een-dee-REE-tsoh dee POH-stah-eh-leht-TROH-nee-kah?*

Italians use and understand both: the Italian words **posta elettronica** and the English one "e-mail."

Can you do e-mail in English / Italian?

Puoi mandare e-mail in inglese / italiano?
pwoy mahn-DAH-reh e-mail een een-GLEH-seh / ee-tah-LYAH-noh?

It's hard to e-mail with this phone.

È difficile mandare e-mail con questo telefono.
eh deef-fee-CHEE-leh mahn-DAH-reh e-mail kohn KWEH-stoh teh-LEH-foh-noh.

But I can send instant messages.

Ma posso mandare messaggini.
mah POHS-soh mahn-DAH-reh meh-sah-DJEE-nee.

Could you teach me?

Mi puoi insegnare?
mee pwoy een-seh-NYAH-reh?

The **gn** is pronounced like the **ni** in the English word "onion."

I'll send you a text
   message later.

**Ti mando un messaggino
dopo.**

*tee mahn-doh oon meh-sah-
DJEE-noh DOH-poh.*

You will hear this sentence all the time, as this has become
the way to confirm appointments, dates, timing, last minute
cancellations: with a **messaggino**. And as in other countries,
the **messaggini** have a new, abbreviated language all their
own.

How are you doing?

Come stai?
KOH-meh stah-ee?

I've been doing okay.

Sono stato bene.
SOH-noh STAH-toh BEH-neh.

What were you doing?

Cosa stavi facendo.
*KOH-zah STAH-vee
fah-CHEHN-doh.*

You are late.

Sei in ritardo.
seh-ee een ree-TAHR-doh.

I tried to call you.

Ho cercato di chiamarti.
*oh chehr-KAH-toh dee
kyah-MAHR-tee.*

I could not find you.

Non ti ho trovato.
nohn tee oh troh-VAH-toh.

The line was busy.

Il telefono era occupato.
*eel teh-LEH-foh-noh eh-rah
ohk-koo-PAH-toh.*

My (phone) battery was low.   **Avevo le batterie scariche (del telefonino).**
*ah-VEH-voh leh baht-teh-REE-eh SKAH-ree-keh
(dehl teh-leh-foh-NEE-noh).*

If someone says something like this to you, it's a red flag: in Italy people do not forget to charge their cell phones. Also there are basically no areas of the country where you cannot get reception. Italians have worked very hard to build efficient infrastructures that allow them to "never lose touch" with each other.

Who was on the phone?   **Chi era al telefono?**
kee eh-rah ahl teh-LEH-foh-noh?

I want to see you.   **Ti voglio vedere.**
tee VOH-lyoh veh-DEH-reh.

I'll call you again.   **Ti richiamerò.**
tee ree-kyah-meh-ROH.

I'll call you after I get there.   **Ti chiamo quando arrivo.**
tee KYAH-moh KWAHN-doh ahr-REE-voh.

What time can I call tomorrow?   **A che ora posso chiamare domani?**
ah keh OH-rah POHS-soh kyah-MAH-reh doh-MAH-nee?

I'll call tomorrow at
   6 o'clock.

**Chiamo domani alle sei in
   punto.**
*KYAH-moh doh-MAH-nee ahl-
   leh seh-ee een POON-toh.*

Please be home.

Per favore fatti trovare.
*pehr fah-VOH-reh FAHT-tee
   troh-VAH-reh.*

Will you be checking
   your e-mail tomorrow?

**Controllerai la tua e-mail
   domani?**
*kohn-troh-leh-RAH-ee lah TOO-
   ah e-mail doh-MAH-nee?*

Say hello to Chiara for me.

Dì ciao a Chiara per me.
*dee chah-oh ah Chiara
   pehr meh.*

Chitchat and Courting
Chiacchiere e Corteggiamento

Are you having a good time?	**Ti stai divertendo?** *tee stah-ee* *dee-vehr-TEHN-doh?*

You will use and overhear this word a lot, in these forms: **divertire** (to cheer up, to entertain), **divertirsi** (the reflexive form, "to amuse one*self*") and the adjective **divertente**. Italians use all these to define many things. Activities, people, situations, even clothing, can all be described as **divertenti**.

You look like you are having a good time.	**Sembra che tu ti stia divertendo.** *SEHM-brah keh too tee stee-ah dee-vehr-TEHN-doh.*
Yeah, I am having fun.	**Sì, mi sto divertendo.** *see, mee stoh dee-vehr-TEHN-doh.*
No, not really.	**Veramente no.** *veh-rah-MEHN-teh noh.*
We are having a good time, aren't we?	**Noi ci stiamo divertendo, vero?** *nwoy chee STYAH-moh dee-vehr-TEHN-doh, VEH-roh?*

Did you two come here by yourselves?	**Voi due siete venute/i qui da sole/i? / Siete sole?** *vwoy DOO-eh SYEH-teh veh-NOO-teh/tee kwee dah SOH-leh/lee? / SYEH-teh SOH-leh?*

Italians often use the second, abbreviated form, "**Siete sole?**" (Are you by yourselves?).

Shall we drink together?	**Beviamo qualcosa insieme?** *beh-VYAH-moh kwahl-KOH-zah een-SYEH-meh?*

Yet again, a reminder: the same sentence can be interrogative or affirmative. It all depends on the tone of voice. You can say the words "**Beviamo qualcosa insieme**" as a statement, or as question. Repeat after the Italians: use your voice and your body carefully, and they will understand which one you mean.

Has someone reserved this seat? / Is someone sitting here?	**È prenotato questo posto? / È libera questa sedia?** *eh preh-noh-TAH-toh KWEH-stoh POH-stoh? / eh LEE-beh-rah KWEH-stah SEH-dyah?*

Italians usually use the word **posto** ("place"), instead of a literal "seat" (**sedia**). **Posto** indicates many different things: a chair, a table, a room, a beach chair, a seat at the movie, and so on.

In a restaurant, though, it is customary to ask "**È prenotato questo tavolo?**", using the word "table."

Do you want to sit down?	**Vuoi sederti?** *vwoy seh-DEHR-tee?*

May I sit down?

Posso sedermi?
POHS-soh seh-DEHR-mee?

Let me sit down.

Fammi sedere.
FAHM-mee seh-DEH-reh.

Shuffle over / make room.

Fammi posto.
FAHM-mee POH-stoh.

Do you like this music?

Ti piace questa musica?
tee PYAH-cheh KWEH-stah MOO-see-kah?

What music do you like?

Quale musica ti piace?
KWAH-leh MOO-see-kah tee PYAH-cheh?

Whose music do you like?

Quali sono i tuoi cantanti preferiti?
KWAH-lee SOH-noh ee too-ee kahn-TAHN-tee preh-feh-REE-tee?

Do you know this song?

Conosci questa canzone?
koh-NOH-shee KWEH-stah kahn-TSOH-neh?

I know it.

La conosco.
lah koh-NOH-skoh.

I don't know it.	**Non la conosco.** *nohn lah koh-NOH-skoh.*
Shall we dance?	**Balliamo?** *bahl-LYAH-moh?*

Remember: everything is in your tone of voice. The same sentence, "**Balliamo,**" can sound like a command, an invitation, or a question.

I don't feel like dancing yet.	**Non ho voglia di ballare per ora.** *nohn oh VOH-lyah dee bahl- LAH-reh pehr oh-rah.*
You're a good dancer.	**Sei un/una bravo/a ballerino/a.** *seh-ee oon/oon-ah brah-voh/ vah bahl-leh-REE-noh/nah.*
How do you know of this place?	**Come conosci questo posto?** *KOH-meh koh-NOH-shee KWEH-stoh POH-stoh?*
I heard from my friends.	**Degli amici lo conoscevano.** *DEH-lyee ah-MEE-chee loh koh-noh-SHEH-vah-noh.*
Where else do you go to dance?	**Vai a ballare in altri posti / discoteche?** *vah-ee ah bahl-LAH-reh een AHL-tree POH-stee / dee-skoh-TEH-keh?*

In Italy the most popular places to go dancing are private homes—where dancing **feste** (parties) are still very common especially among young people—and the **discoteche** (disco clubs). In most towns, and especially in summer vacation villages, there are plenty of **discoteche**. In many cities you will also find piano bars, more elegant places where you sit at a bar or on sofas while someone plays the piano and sings. There are also private clubs, and of course hotel lounges.

How long have you been in Italy?	**Quanto tempo sei stato in Italia?** *KWAHN-toh TEHM-poh seh-ee STAH-toh een ee-TAH-lyah?*
Let's party!	**Andiamo ad una festa / Facciamo una festa!** *ahn-DYAH-moh ahd oo-nah FEHS-tah / fah-CHYAH-moh oo-nah FEHS-tah.*

There is no real equivalent of the English "Let's party." But the word **festa**, "party," implies having good music and dancing. **Fare una festa** means to organize a party, while **Andiamo a una festa** means "Let's go to a party" and it can be used when in fact this is the plan.

Italians could also say "**Divertiamoci**" ("Let's have fun"), which would almost always involve having good food to accompany whatever fun activities are chosen. The concept of **divertirsi** when you are not busy with your duties, is a way of living in Italy…Italians believe that enjoying life is an art to perfect.

As an example, in Italy no one gives up their vacation time as happens more and more in America; Italian cities are emptied in the summer. Even the most workaholic Italians will take 20 to 30 days off. If you spend August in Rome or in Milan, you'll feel like you're in a ghost town.

Let's enjoy life!   **Godiamoci la vita!**
                                   goh-dyah-MOH-chee
                                   lah VEE-tah!

Getting back to "partying" in an actual nightclub where people are drinking a lot, or in **una osteria**—a sort of bar that sells almost only wines—the following phrases will be very useful.

Let's get drunk!   **Ubriachiamoci!**
                                  oo-bryah-kyah-MOH-chee!

What are you drinking?   **Cosa bevi?**
                                  KOH-zah beh-vee?

Have you been drinking   **Hai bevuto molto?**
   a lot?   *ah-ee beh-VOO-toh MOHL-toh?*

You need to drink more.   **Hai bisogno di bere di più.**
                                  ah-ee bee-SOH-nyoh dee
                                  BEH-reh dee pyoo.

Are you drunk?   **Sei ubriaco/a?**
                                  seh-ee oo-BRYAH-koh/kah?

Haven't you drunk   **Non hai bevuto troppo?**
   too much?   *nohn ah-ee beh-VOO-toh*
                                  TROHP-poh?

Maybe you should stop drinking.	**Dovresti smettere di bere adesso.** *doh-VREH-stee SMEHT-teh-reh dee BEH-reh ah-DEHS-soh.*
Are you okay?	**Stai bene?** *stah-ee BEH-neh?*
You are kind.	**Sei gentile.** *seh-ee jehn-TEE-leh.*
What time did you come here?	**A che ora sei venuto/a qui?** *ah kay OH-rah seh-ee veh-NOO-toh/tah kwee?*
What time is your curfew?	**A che ora è il tuo coprifuoco?** *ah kay OH-rah eh eel too-oh koh-pree-FWOH-koh?*
What time are you leaving?	**A che ora te ne andrai?** *ah kay OH-rah teh neh ahn-DRAH-ee?*
I haven't decided.	**Non ho deciso.** *nohn oh deh-CHEE-zoh.*
If I have a good time I'll stay.	**Se mi diverto, resterò.** *seh mee dee-VEHR-toh, reh-steh-ROH.*
If this gets boring, I'll go home.	**Se mi annoio, andrò a casa.** *seh mee ahn-NWOH-yoh, ahn-DROH ah KAH-zah.*

I'll help you to have
a good time.

Ti aiuto a divertirti.
*tee ah-YOO-toh
ah dee-vehr-TEER-tee.*

This is boring!

**Che noia / Mi annoio /
Mi rompo.**
*kay NWOH-yah /
mee ahn-NWOH-yoh /
mee ROHM-poh.*

The first two sentences can be used interchangeably, and are typical in polite Italian language. The third one, **mi rompo**, is very colloquial and you will hear it a lot. It has sexual connotations—it literally means "I am breaking my balls"—but it is not considered vulgar in Italian; in fact even well-educated people use it in everyday conversations.

Shall we go somewhere else?

**Andiamo da qualche altra
parte?**
*ahn-DYAH-moh dah KWAHL-
keh AHL-trah PAHR-teh?*

Shall we leave?

Ce ne andiamo?
chay neh ahn-DYAH-moh?

Can my friends come?

Possono venire i miei amici?
*POHS-soh-noh veh-NEE-reh ee
MYEH-ee ah-MEE-chee?*

When you speak generally about friends you use the plural masculine form (**amici** to indicate male friends, or a mix of male and female friends). To indicate a group of female friends you would say "**amiche**" instead.

I'd like to stay longer.

Vorrei stare di più.
VOHR-reh STAH-reh dee pyoo.

What's next?

Cosa facciamo dopo?
*KOH-zah fah-CHYAH-moh
DOH-poh?*

Have you decided?

Hai deciso?
ah-ee deh-CHEE-zoh?

I haven't decided yet.

Non ho ancora deciso.
*nohn oh ahn-KOH-rah
deh-CHEE-zoh.*

It's up to you.

Dipende da te.
dee-PEHN-deh dah teh.

Anything is fine.

Va bene tutto.
vah BEH-neh TOOT-toh.

I have a good idea.

Ho una buona idea.
*oh oo-nah BWOH-nah
ee-DAY-ah.*

How does that sound?

Cosa ne pensi?
KOH-zah neh PEHN-see?

Good idea!

Buona idea!
BWOH-nah ee-DAY-ah!

Anywhere is okay.

Va bene ovunque.
vah BEH-neh oh-VOON-kweh.

I'll take you home.

Ti porto a casa.
tee POHR-toh ah KAH-zah.

LA CORTE

The following are phrases that can be used at the beginning of a nice courtship...

I want to know more about you.

Voglio conoscerti di più / meglio.
VOH-lyoh koh-noh-SHEHR-tee dee pyoo / MEH-lyoh.

I like talking to you.

Mi piace parlare con te.
mee PYAH-cheh pahr-LAH-reh kohn teh.

You are so beautiful.

Sei così bella/o.
seh-ee koh-ZEE BEHL-lah/loh.

We think the same way, don't we? / We are so similar.

Pensiamo allo stesso modo / Siamo così simili.
pehn-SYAH-moh AHL-loh STEHS-soh MOH-doh / SYAH-moh koh-ZEE SEE-mee-lee.

Shall we see each other again?

Ti va se ci vediamo ancora?
tee vah seh chee veh-DYAH-moh ahn-KOH-rah?

Let's see each other again.

Vediamoci ancora.
veh-dyah-MOH-chee ahn-KOH-rah.

I enjoyed myself.

Sono stato/a bene.
SOH-noh STAH-toh/tah BEH-neh.

When can I see you next time?	**Quando ti posso vedere la prossima volta?** *KWAHN-doh tee POHS-soh veh-DEH-reh lah PROHS-see-mah VOHL-tah?*
Do you want to drink a coffee together tomorrow?	**Ci vediamo per un caffè domani?** *chee veh-DYAH-moh pehr oon kahf-FEH doh-MAH-nee?*
May I call you?	**Ti posso chiamarei?** *tee POHS-soh kyah-MAH-reh-ee?*
May I have your phone number?	**Mi dai il tuo numero di telefono?** *mee dah-ee eel too-oh NOO-meh-roh dee teh-LEH-foh-noh?*
Do you have something to write with?	**Hai una penna?** *ah-ee oo-nah PEHN-nah?*
Take care.	**Stai bene.** *stah-ee BEH-neh.*
See you later.	**Ci vediamo.** *chee veh-DYAH-moh.*

Ci vediamo is one of the 100 most used sentences in Italy. It is informal, it is friendly, it is everyday language, but it can also be used with colleagues at the end of a work day, with a husband, a sister, a best friend or the doorman. It gives that special all-Italian meaning that not only will you see each other again soon, but that the communication channel remains always open. You don't even need to specify when you'll see each other again, you are just sure it will happen. **Ci vediamo** is just a fact: "We'll see each other," period.

See you tomorrow.

Ci vediamo domani.
chee veh-DYAH-moh
doh-MAH-nee.

Lovers' Language
La Lingua dell'Amore 12

I like you.	**Mi piaci.** *mee PYAH-chee.*
I like you very much.	**Mi piaci molto.** *mee PYAH-chee MOHL-toh.*
I am attracted to you.	**Mi attrai.** *mee aht-TRAH-ee.*
I feel good being with you.	**Sto bene quando sono con te.** *stoh BEH-neh KWAHN-doh SOH-noh kohn teh.*
I am crazy about you.	**Sono pazzo / pazza di te.** *SOH-noh PAH-tsoh / PAH-tsah dee teh.*

(Say "**pazzo**" if you are male; "**pazza**" if you are female.) This sentence can often be used with a smile, as a way to say something actually true to a partner while making it look like you are exaggerating your own feelings. In one way or another, more or less true to their authentic feelings, Italians use this phrase a lot.

I love you.	**Ti amo.** *tee AH-moh.*

I adore you.   **Ti adoro.**
                                tee ah-DOH-roh.

Remember: the concept of adoration and the related verbs/words are not "restricted" in Italy to religion. Italians happily "adore" a lot of things and persons in their life.

I'm yours.   **Sono tuo / tua.**
                                SOH-noh TOO-oh / TOO-ah.

Say the first if you're male; say the second if you're female.

You are mine.   **Sei mio / mia.**
                                seh-ee MEE-oh / MEE-ah.

Say the first if you're telling a male; say the second if you're telling a female.

I want to know all   **Voglio sapere tutto**
   about you.   **di te.**
                                VOH-lyoh sah-PEH-reh
                                TOOT-toh dee teh.

I'll tell you.   **Ti dirò tutto.**
                                tee dee-ROH TOOT-toh.

You look beautiful.   **Sei bella/o.**
                                seh-ee BEHL-lah/loh.

You are attractive /   **Sei attraente / sei sexy.**
   you are sexy.   *seh-ee aht-trah-EHN-teh /*
                                seh-ee sexy.

"Sexy" is a word in very common use in Italy, even more so than the authentic Italian word **attraente**.

Look at me.   **Guardami.**
                                GWAHR-dah-mee.

You have beautiful eyes.

Hai dei begli occhi.
ah-ee deh-ee BEH-lyee OH-kee.

I want to be close to you.

Voglio starti vicino / vicina.
VOH-lyoh STAHR-tee vee-
CHEE-noh / vee-CHEE-nah.

Say the first if you're male; say the second if you're female.

May I kiss you?

Posso baciarti?
POHS-soh bah-CHYAHR-tee?

Kiss me.

Baciami.
bah-CHYAH-mee.

May I love you?

Posso amarti?
POHS-soh ah-MAHR-tee?

I want to hold you tight.

Voglio tenerti stretto/a.
VOH-lyoh teh-NEHR-tee STRE-
HT-toh/tah.

I want to come and visit
you in America.

Voglio venire a trovarti
in America.
VOH-lyoh veh-NEE-reh ah
troh-VAHR-tee een
ah-MEH-ree-kah.

I want to come back to Italy for you.

Voglio tornare in Italia per te.
VOH-lyoh tohr-NAH-reh een ee-TAH-lyah pehr teh.

I want to stay with you forever.

Voglio stare con te per sempre.
VOH-lyoh stah-reh kohn teh pehr SEHM-preh.

Shall we think about getting married?

Parliamo di matrimonio?
pahr-LYAH-moh dee mah-tree-MOH-nyoh?

I'm not ready to talk about marriage yet.

Non sono pronto a parlare di matrimonio.
nohn SON-noh PROHN-toh ah pahr-LAH-reh dee mah-tree-MOH-nyoh.

Will you marry me?

Mi vuoi sposare?
mee vwoy spoh-SAH-reh?

I don't want to get married yet.

Non voglio sposarmi per ora.
nohn VOH-lyoh spoh-SAHR-mee pehr OH-rah.

Don't get me wrong.

Non pensare male di me.
*nohn pehn-SAH-reh MAH-leh
dee meh.*

I love you but I can't
marry you.

**Ti amo ma non posso
sposarti.**
*tee AH-moh mah nohn POHS-
soh spoh-SAHR-tee.*

It's not time for me to
get serious.

**Non è il momento giusto
per un rapporto serio
per me.**
*nohn eh eel moh-MEHN-toh
JOO-stoh pehr oon
rahp-POHR-toh SEH-ryoh
pehr meh.*

I am not good for you.

Non vado bene per te.
*nohn VAH-doh BEH-neh
pehr teh.*

Forget about me.

Dimenticami.
dee-MEHN-tee-kah-mee.

I need time to myself.

**Ho bisogno di tempo per
me.**
*oh bee-SOH-nyoh dee
TEHM-poh pehr meh.*

I'll be in touch.

Ti chiamerò.
tee kyah-meh-ROH.

Love that Comes, Love that Goes
Amore che Viene, Amore che Va

I am sorry it didn't work out.	**Mi dispiace che non ha funzionato tra noi.** *mee dees-PYAH-cheh kay nohn ah foon-tsyoh-NAH-toh trah nwoy.*
It's over.	**È finita.** *eh fee-NEE-tah.*
Don't be persistent.	**Non insistere.** *nohn een-see-STEH-reh.*
I don't want to see you anymore.	**Non voglio più vederti.** *nohn VOH-lyoh pyoo veh-DEHR-tee.*
Do you have another boyfriend / girlfriend?	**Hai un altro ragazzo / ragazza?** *ah-ee oon AHL-troh rah-GAH-tsoh / rah-GAH-tsah?*
I have another boyfriend / girlfriend.	**Ho un altro ragazzo / ragazza.** *oh oon AHL-troh rah-GAH-tsoh / rah-GAH-tsah.*

I won't call you anymore.

Non ti chiamerò più.
nohn tee kyah-meh-ROH pyoo.

I can't see you anymore.

Non posso più vederti.
nohn POHS-soh pyoo
veh-DEHR-tee.

I'm not interested in you
anymore.

Non mi interessi più.
nohn mee een-teh-REHS-see
pyoo.

Being with you is not fun.

**Stare con te non è
divertente.**
STAH-reh kohn teh nohn eh
dee-vehr-TEHN-teh.

Stop bothering me.

Smettila di seccarmi.
SMEHT-tee-lah dee
seh-KAHR-mee.

You don't love me anymore,
do you?

Tu non mi ami più, vero?
too nohn mee AH-mee pyoo,
VEH-roh?

I don't like you anymore.

Non mi piaci più.
nohn mee PYAH-chee pyoo.

It's my fault.

È colpa mia.
eh KOHL-pah MEE-ah.

I'm sorry, I haven't been
a good boyfriend /
girlfriend.

Mi dispiace non sono stato/a
un buon ragazzo/a
per te.
mee dees-PYAH-cheh nohn
SOH-noh STAH-toh/tah oon
bwohn rah-GAH-tsoh/tsah
pehr teh.

Please understand my
feelings.

Per favore cerca di capire i
miei sentimenti.
pehr fah-VOH-reh CHER-kah
dee kah-PEE-reh
ee MYEH-ee
sehn-tee-MEHN-tee.

I'll never forget you.

Non ti dimenticherò mai.
nohn tee dee-mehn-tee-cheh-
ROH mah-ee.

I'm so happy to have
known you.

Sono felice di averti
conosciuto/a.
SOH-noh feh-LEE-cheh dee
ah-VEHR-tee koh-noh-
SHOO-toh/tah.

Say the first if you're telling a male; say the second if you're
telling a female.

Remember me sometimes.

Ricordati di me qualche
volta.
ree-kohr-DAH-tee dee meh
KWAHL-kay VOHL-tah.

Can we still be friends?

Possiamo essere ancora amici?
poh-SYAH-moh ehs-SEH-reh ahn-KOH-rah ah-MEE-chee?

Let's start again.

Ricominciamo.
ree-koh-meen-CHYAH-moh.

I will always love you.

Ti amerò sempre.
tee ah-meh-ROH SEHM-preh.

Can't we start again?

Possiamo cominciare di nuov?
poh-SYAH-moh koh-meen-CHYAH-reh dee nwohv?

I am serious about you.

Sono serio / seria con te.
SOH-noh SEH-ryoh / SEH-ryah kohn teh.

Say the first if you're male; say the second if you're female.

I can't live without you.

Non posso vivere senza di te.
nohn POHS-soh vee-VEH-reh SEHN-tsah dee teh.

I'm so happy to have known you.

Sono così felice di averti incontrato/a.
SOH-noh koh-ZEE feh-LEE-cheh dee ah-VEHR-tee een-kohn-TRAH-toh/tah.

Say the first if you're telling a male; say the second if you're telling a female.

I'll miss you.

Mi mancherai.
mee mahn-cheh-RAH-ee.

I'll always think of you.

Ti penserò sempre.
tee pehn-seh-ROH SEHM-preh.

I'll write you letters.

Ti scriverò.
tee skree-veh-ROH.

Will you write me letters?

Mi scriverai?
mee skree-veh-RAH-ee?

I'll call you when I return.

Ti chiamerò quando torno.
tee kyah-meh-ROH kwahn-doh TOHR-noh.

I have to go because of my job.

Devo andare per il mio lavoro.
DEH-voh ahn-DAH-reh pehr eel mee-oh lah-VOH-roh.

Please wait for my return.

Per favore aspetta il mio ritorno.
pehr fah-VOH-reh ah-SPEHT-tah eel mee-oh ree-TOHR-noh.

Don't cry.

Non piangere.
nohn pyahn-JEH-reh.

Wipe your tears.

Asciugati le lacrime.
ah-shoo-GAH-tee leh
LAH-kree-meh.

Take care of yourself.

Prenditi cura di te.
PREHN-dee-tee KOO-rah
dee teh.

I'll be back soon.

Tornerò presto.
tohr-neh-ROH PREH-stoh.